Landmarks of world literatu

Giovanni Boccaccio

DECAMERON

Landmarks of world literature

General Editor: J. P. Stern

GIOVANNI BOCCACCIO

Decameron

DAVID WALLACE

Paul W. Frenzel Chair in Medieval Studies,
University of Minnesota

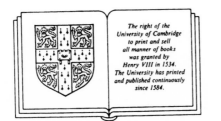

CAMBRIDGE UNIVERSITY PRESS

Cambridge
New York   Port Chester
Melbourne   Sydney

Published by the Press Syndicate of the University of Cambridge
The Pitt Building, Trumpington Street, Cambridge CB2 1RP
40 West 20th Street, New York, NY 10011-4211, USA
10 Stamford Road, Oakleigh, Melbourne 3166, Australia

First published 1991

British Library cataloguing in publication data
Wallace, David *1954–*
Giovanni Boccaccio: *Decameron* – (Landmarks of world
literature).
1. Italian literature. Boccaccio, Giovanni, 1313–75
I. Title   II. Series 858.109

Library of Congress cataloging in publication data
Wallace, David (David J.)
Giovanni Boccaccio, *Decameron* / David Wallace.
      p.   cm. – (Landmarks of world literature).
Includes bibliographical references.
ISBN 0 521 38182 7 – ISBN 0 521 38851 1 (pbk)
1. Boccaccio, Giovanni, 1313–75. *Decameron.*   I. Series.
PQ4287.W35   1991
853'.1 – dc20   90–28232   CIP

ISBN 0 521 38182 7 hardback
ISBN 0 521 38851 1 paperback

Transferred to digital printing 2003

for here and there:
Rita Copeland
and
Robin Kirkpatrick

Contents

viii   DECAMERON

Acknowledgments

References to the *Decameron* follow the text in *Tutte le opere di Giovanni Boccaccio*, ed. Vittore Branca, 12 vols., incomplete (Milan, 1964–), vol. IV. Quotations in English follow the Penguin translation of G. H. McWilliam (Harmondsworth, 1972) unless otherwise indicated.

I would like to thank the National Endowment for the Humanities and the University of Texas Research Institute for financial support. This book was written in two collegial settings that Boccaccio would have approved of: the National Humanities Center, North Carolina and St Edmund's College, Cambridge. It has benefited much from the criticisms of Dino Cervigni, Robin Kirkpatrick, Millicent Marcus, Glending Olson, Joy Hambuechen Potter and J. P. Stern.

Chronology

Boccaccio's life and works

(*Note*: most datings of literary works are approximate)

1313	Boccaccio born
1321	
1327	Joins father at Naples, becomes apprentice merchant or *discepolo* of the Bardi company
1330–31	Switches to study of canon law (and studies Latin classics)
1334	*Caccia di Diana*
1335	*Filostrato*
1337	
1338	Completes *Filocolo*
1340	Returns to Florence (winter 1340–1)
1341	Completes text and glosses of *Teseida*
1342	Completes *Comedia delle Ninfe, De vita et moribus Domini Francisci Petracchi*
1343	*Amorosa Visione*
1344	*Elegia di Madonna Fiammetta*
1346	Boccaccio lives in Ravenna; *Ninfale Fiesolano*

Historical events

	Emperor Henry VII dies
	Dante dies, 14 September
	Cino da Pistoia teaches civil law at Naples
	Hundred Years War begins
	Plague in Florence: 15,000 die (Villani); abortive *coup* by Bardi and other magnates
	Petrarch crowned Poet Laureate at Rome
	Walter of Brienne *signore* of Florence; birth of Chaucer
	Walter of Brienne expelled from Florence; new Republican regime
	Edward III defaults on loans; Peruzzi and other banks fail
	Edward III defaults; Bardi company fails; famine conditions in Florence

1347	Boccaccio at court of Francesco Ordelaffi, Forlì	Plague in Florence: 4,000 die (Villani)
1348	Returns to Florence; father, stepmother die; becomes head of family; begins *Decameron*	Black Death across Europe; 50,000 of 80,000 Florentines die
1350	Begins *Genealogia deorum gentilium*; sent on diplomatic mission to Romagna; visits Sister Beatrice, Dante's daughter, at Ravenna; meets Petrarch at Florence	Jubilee year; pilgrimages to Rome
1351	Represents Quarter of Santo Spirito, Jan–Feb; Camarlengo (bursar) of the Chamber of the Commune, delegate of the Signoria; sent on mission to Ludwig of Bavaria to discuss intervention against the Visconti; *Trattatello in laude di Dante*, version I; completes *Decameron*	Florence at war with Milan (until 1353)
1352	Sent to Padua to offer Petrarch return of patrimony and chair at Florentine Studio (university)	Petrarch refuses Florentine offers; moves to Avignon
1353	Mission to Forlì and Ravenna, probably to discuss threat of Visconti expansionism	Petrarch accepts Visconti patronage; lives in Milan (until 1361)
1354	Ambassador to Innocent VI at Avignon	First Italian expedition of Emperor Charles IV; Florence threatened
1355	Organizes resistance to mercenary Fra Moriale at Certaldo; oversees mercenary troops in Florence; visits Naples; copies manuscripts at Montecassino; begins *De casibus virorum illustrium*	
1359	Visits Petrarch at Milan	

1360	Promotes teaching of Greek at Florentine Studio and translations from Homer; granted full dispensation from illegitimate birth by Innocent VI; qualifies for ecclesiastical benefices	Truce in Hundred Years War; mercenaries begin descent on Italy; abortive *coup* in Florence
1361	Friends exiled; withdraws to Certaldo (1361–5); *Epistola consolatoria a Pino de' Rossi*; begins *De mulieribus claris*	1363 plague in Florence 1362, 1364 Florence at war with Pisa
1365	*Corbaccio*; resumes political life in Florence: ambassador to Urban V	Christine de Pisan born, Venice
1367	Consulted on building of tabernacle at Or San Michele; visits Venice; probably meets Philippe de Mézières; ambassador to Urban V at Rome; oversees mercenaries at Florence	Papacy returns to Italy
1368	Visits Petrarch at Padua (July)	Petrarch attends wedding of Violante Visconti and Lionel, Duke of Clarence at Milan (June 5); second Italian expedition of Charles IV; Florence at war with Milan; Hundred Years War resumes
1369		
1370	Moves to Naples; rumour in Florence that he has become a monk	Urban V returns to Avignon, dies, succeeded by Gregory XI
1371	Returns to Florence; recopies and revises *Decameron*	
1373	Revised, enlarged edition of *De casibus*; begins lectures on Dante (23 October)	Chaucer in Florence
1374		Petrarch dies at Arquà, 18 July
1375	Visited by Coluccio Salutati at Certaldo; dies at Certaldo, 21 December	Salutati becomes Chancellor of Florentine Republic; Florence at war with papacy

| 1377 | Death of Machaut, Edward III |
| 1378 | Fall of Florentine regime in Ciompi rebellion; death of Galeazzo Visconti; Chaucer in Lombardy; papal schism |

Chapter 1

The making of the *Decameron*

The *Decameron* as a landmark of world literature

Boccaccio's *Decameron* was occasioned by the greatest natural disaster in European history: the Black Death, a combination of bubonic, pneumonic, and septicaemic plague strains which, between 1347 and 1351, killed off between one quarter and one half of the European population. Millions also died in China and India; the entire Islamic world was engulfed by the plague by 1349 and one third of its population perished. By the late spring of 1350 between 35 percent and 40 percent (perhaps as many as 50 percent) of Londoners had died. Avignon, then the home of the papacy, buried 11,000 people in a single graveyard in one six-week period, lost at least one third of its cardinals and half its population. Scandinavia lost half of its people, Iceland perhaps 60 percent; Christian settlement in Greenland came to an end altogether. Estimates of the deathrate in Boccaccio's Florence range from 45 percent to 75 percent. Boccaccio saw his own father and his stepmother die. Suddenly, at the age of thirty-five (the mid-life age, *nel mezzo del cammin*, at which Dante stages the journey of his *Commedia*) Boccaccio found himself head of his own household in a city where the familiar forms of civilized life (which for a Florentine were synonymous with *civic* life) had come to an end.

The organizing framework of the *Decameron* takes shape as seven young women and three young men agree to withdraw from Florence and wait out the plague in the nearby hills of Fiesole. Each of the ten members of this company, or *brigata*, reigns as monarch for one day; each person tells one story, or *novella*, per day. By the end of two weeks, which allows for ten days of story-telling, one hundred *novelle* have

1

been told and the 'decameron' is complete (Boccaccio's title, which means 'of the ten days', combines the Greek terms δέκα and ἡμερῶν). The *Decameron* was an immediate success with the merchant and entrepreneurial classes that figure so largely in its *novelle*: some of the early manuscripts that were so eagerly copied and circulated bear traces of business accounts, loans and rentals in their margins. Although the early Florentine humanists were not prepared to recognize a collection of tales in Italian prose as a serious work of literature (serious works were written in Latin), the *Decameron* quickly reached an international audience: soon after Boccaccio's death in 1375, Franco Sacchetti (Boccaccio's most important successor as a Florentine *novelliere*) speaks of the *Decameron* being translated into French and English (no Middle English translation survives); translations into Catalan, German and Spanish ensured that Boccaccio's work exerted a significant influence on emergent vernacular traditions. Whereas the *Chanson de Roland*, the *Divine Comedy* and *The Canterbury Tales* tended to circulate within delimited social groupings or discrete national cultures, Boccaccio's *novelle* found a much broader audience across a greater geographical range. The *Decameron* is the first landmark text of modern times to exert a truly European influence.

The instant and enduring popularity of the *Decameron* is due to the energy and versatility of its style and the originality of its form. Boccaccio achieves a new kind of literary language, a prose that escapes the formative constraints of its Latin models and yet draws from them sufficient subtlety, rhythmic variety and complexity to map out new areas of human experience. He sometimes (most often in opening a new *novella*) writes with a constraint and balance reminiscent of Dante's *Convivio*; and sometimes (when a *novella* is in full flow) with a simulated abandon that suggests the spontaneity of colloquial speech rather than the discipline of writing, *parola* rather than *scrittura*. Boccaccio sometimes imitates and sometimes parodies the full range of medieval genres, from courtly lyric and *chanson de geste* to saint's life and fabliau. And yet (unlike Chaucer) he chooses to contain such encyclopaedic variety within the limits of a single, stabilized genre, the *novella*. These short prose narratives are set in sequence by an organizing frame or *cornice* which transforms a mixed bag of tales into a unitary work of art. Boccaccio's *novelle* sequence thus becomes the prototype of the modern novel; its literary line of descent extends beyond the Middle Ages and Renaissance to connect novelists as diverse as Manzoni, Lawrence and Faulkner.

The content of the *Decameron*, like its style and form, assumes a historical importance that extends far beyond the occasion of the plague. For even when Boccaccio's *novelle* attempt to evoke the time-honoured feudal, hierarchic or hierocratic values of earlier societies they typically discover their difference from them, a difference that is sometimes experienced as nostalgia, sometimes as loss, and is sometimes imperfectly assimilated into the narrative logic of storytelling and its accepted forms of closure. In departing from traditional medieval strategies of experiencing and explaining the world, the *Decameron* establishes itself as a prophetic text for centuries to come. This explains, of course, why it becomes a text of first resort for writers across Europe long after Chaucer and Dante have been abandoned as medieval curiosities. Without committing ourselves to a reductive, deterministic, base and superstructure model of historical explanation, we can acknowledge that the precociousness of Boccaccio's text stands in some relation to the precociousness of mid-fourteenth-century Florence. Florence at this time boasted a Republican polity more broad based and socially inclusive than virtually any other regime of the medieval and Renaissance periods. This society, the society of the *Decameron*'s first readership, struggled to equilibrate economic and political forces that were barely stirring in other areas of Europe and would not be fully developed for hundreds of years. Such forces achieved expression through the new-found powers of capital, the rapid expansion of mercantile enterprise and the emergent ideology of the territorial (city and nation) state.

Few texts, then, offer more authentic landmark credentials

than Boccaccio's *Decameron*. The occasion which prompted its writing was itself one of the most momentous events of world history: the Black Death was a demographic disaster which brought far-reaching social and economic changes in the West and brought on new forms of disaster, such as the persecution of minority populations (held responsible for the epidemic) and the beginnings of the black slave trade. The *Decameron* responded to the needs of a politically precocious society with a language and organizational form that would answer to European experience for many centuries to come. It also represents both the midpoint and high point of Boccaccio's career. After the *Decameron* Boccaccio devoted himself to the civic life of Florence, Latin encyclopaedism and the incipient humanist movement; very little of his time was given to writing in Italian. Before the *Decameron* Boccaccio wrote a good deal in the vernacular, although his early writings are more often studied as sources for Chaucer than as works of independent merit. But Boccaccio's formative years do warrant some attention if we are to understand how and why everything comes together so seamlessly – history and politics, genre and style – in the moment of the *Decameron*.

Boccaccio, Naples and Florence before the *Decameron*

Boccaccio was born during the summer of 1313, perhaps in the small village of Certaldo in the rural hinterland of Florence, but more probably in Florence itself. It is not known who his mother was. In his *Filocolo* Boccaccio suggests that he was born of a French princess, seduced by his father during a business trip to Paris. This legend (elaborated and revered for some five hundred years) reflects Boccaccio's youthful admiration for French culture but has no factual basis. Boccaccio's father, Boccaccino, was a successful merchant who held a number of civic offices in Florence and was appointed as one of the eight priors of the Signoria (the supreme executive office of the Florentine commune) for the usual two-month term in December 1322. Five years later Boccaccino became chief representative of the Bardi, the most famous of all the Florentine merchant and banking companies, at Naples. Boccaccio moved south to join his father in the Florentine merchant colony at Naples in 1327.

During the reign of King Robert the Wise (1309–43) Naples boasted a richness and variety of social, cultural and literary influences that no other European city could rival. The Neapolitan Angevin dynasty was established in 1260 when Charles d'Anjou defeated the Swabian Manfred and became Carlo I of Naples. Charles d'Anjou was a poet and a patron of poets; Sordello and other troubadours followed him to Naples, Adam de la Halle entered his service there around 1283 and Jean de Meun sang the praises of his adopted city in his continuation of the *Roman de la Rose*. French culture was still firmly rooted there in Boccaccio's time, although King Robert was most concerned to encourage Latin learning. He made determined efforts to expand his library and encouraged a succession of important astronomers, encyclopaedists, and scholastic commentators to move to the Angevin capital. Boccaccio first developed his life-long love of Latin learning in the company of these scholars and soon abandoned his career as an apprentice merchant in favour of studying canon law (and the Latin classics) at the Neapolitan Studio. One of the most distinguished professors of law at the Studio was Cino da Pistoia, one of the last poets of the *stil nuovo* and a personal friend of Dante. Cino gave Boccaccio privileged access both to his own lyric poetry and to his epistolary correspondence with Dante.

Boccaccio's first important composition, the *Caccia di Diana*, gives early notice of his extraordinary ability to synthesize diverse and divergent literary sources: in eighteen cantos of Dantean *terza rima*, it echoes a long Latin debate tradition that pits Venus against Diana and parallels a number of closely contemporary hunting poems, such as Jehan Acart de Hesdin's *Prise amoreuse* and Raimon Vidal's *Chasse aux médisants*. His next two poems, the *Filostrato* (source of Chaucer's *Troilus and Criseyde*) and the *Teseida* (source of *The Knight's Tale*), are developed and refined from a popular, oral-derived tradition of stanzaic narrative known as the *cantare*, which has much in common with English tail-rhyme romance. The *Filostrato* isolates and elaborates the tragic love affair of Troiolo and Criseida from a wide range of French, Latin and Italian accounts of the siege of Troy. In his prose preface, Boccaccio (then in his early twenties) addresses his lady and identifies himself with Troiolo, the Trojan prince: the story, Boccaccio says, functions like a *scudo* or shield that covers the sad truth of his own unhappy love life but (through the activity of storytelling) allows some relief for his overcharged emotions. The *Teseida* is a more serious and ambitious affair which reflects Boccaccio's diligent reading of the Latin poet Statius on 'the matter of Thebes'. The *Teseida*'s twelve Books come equipped with erudite glosses and commentary, written by Boccaccio himself; the young Florentine was evidently keen to be perceived as the author of an instant vernacular classic.

The *Filocolo* is a monumentally lengthy retelling of *Fleur et Blancheflor*, the celebrated French romance. In unravelling the endless adventures of Florio (alias Filocolo) and Biancifiore, Boccaccio takes the opportunity to experiment with the stylistic permutations of narrative prose: his schooling in *ars dictaminis* (a rhythmical Latin prose employed in official correspondence) and his translating of classical models such as Livy figure importantly in this stylistic workshop and dress rehearsal for the *Decameron*. In the *Filocolo*'s fourth book, Florio comes across a party of friends or *brigata* debating *questioni d'amore* (questions of love) in a garden near Naples. The fourth narrative in this *questioni* sequence, which was to provide a source for Chaucer's *Franklin's Tale*, was later rewritten (in a compressed and pared-down style) as *Decameron* X, 5. The idyllic gathering of young storytelling aristocrats in the *locus amoenus* of *Filocolo* IV is obviously a prototype of the *Decameron*'s *brigata*.

When Boccaccio returned to Florence in the winter of 1340–1 his writing quickly shifted away from romance and courtly fantasy to address the more serious philosophical and allegorical themes pioneered by the Italianized *Roman de la Rose*, Brunetto Latini and Dante. In the *Amorosa Visione* (*terza rima*) and the *Comedia delle Ninfe* (*terza rima* and prose, a Boethian-style *prosimetrum*), Boccaccio subjects a male protagonist to a systematic education in the ennobling power of love. But in the *Elegia di Madonna Fiammetta* he turns away from allegorical journeys and expert guides to explore the inner world of a Neapolitan woman abandoned by her lover, a young Florentine merchant. In assuming the first-person voice of a woman, Boccaccio reverses the premise of the *Filostrato* (where a woman abandons a man). His attempts to imagine a psychological space that is exclusively female bear comparison with the domestic interiors and female-dominated scenes of Ambrogio and Pietro Lorenzetti (Sienese painters who probably died in the plague of 1348). Both Boccaccio and the Lorenzetti brothers grasp, in different ways, that there are certain areas of female experience that men cannot share. The irony, of course, is that this realization acts as a spur and a challenge to masculine art.

Boccaccio's *Elegia* has been described as the first modern psychological novel. Psychologists might have some interesting things to say about why Boccaccio (and Chaucer after him) feels moved to speak at such length as a female 'I'. But it is more immediately apparent that Boccaccio, through the *Elegia*, is struggling to express some unresolved feelings, some residual unease, at having left Naples for Florence. The leaving of Naples becomes conflated with the loss of childhood: Boccaccio was to make three attempts to return there (the last as an old man in 1370); all three would end in bitterness and disillusion. But without Boccaccio's experience of Naples, and his memories of it, the *Decameron* may never have been written. It would certainly have been a more limited and sombre affair, lacking those aspects of romance and courtly fantasy which nineteenth-century readers (in particular) found so congenial. It would also have missed that remarkable imaginative openness to the greater Mediterranean (Greek and Arab) world, which in Naples formed part of everyday life.

On first returning to Tuscany, Boccaccio may have recalled his life at the fringes of Neapolitan court and Studio society with particular regret, since Florence was then fully embarked on what Gene Brucker has termed 'the decade of disaster' (p. 3). In the spring of 1340 the first of the many plagues that would torment Florence over the next fifty years hit the city while resistance was weakened by famine conditions; the chronicler Giovanni Villani estimated that 15,000 Florentines died. In November of that year the Florentine authorities discovered a plot by several members of the Bardi family to overthrow the regime. All business activity was in a slump: trade with northern Europe was disrupted by the Anglo-French (Hundred Years) war; the Bardi and Peruzzi companies, having financed Edward III's 1340 invasion of France, realized that their position was hopeless once the invasion failed and the king declared his insolvency. In September 1342, backed by desperate magnates, bankers and artisans, the ruling group in Florence attempted to save itself by resorting to *signoria*, or one-man rule. The man they chose was Walter of Brienne, Duke of Athens and nephew of King Robert of Naples. This brought Boccaccio's sentimental attachment to the court-centred culture of Angevin monarchy into direct conflict with his loyalty to the communal values of Republican Florence. Boccaccio remained loyal to the Florentine ideal of self-governing *libertas* throughout this and all later crises; he refused all invitations to join Petrarch at the courts of north Italian despots and was consistently critical of Petrarch for accepting their patronage.

Walter of Brienne was chased out of Florence in July 1343 by a unified effort of all social classes. Boccaccio's friend and correspondent Pino de' Rossi was a leader of this expulsion and (so it seems from the denunciation of Walter's tyranny in Book IV of Boccaccio's *De casibus virorum illustrium*) Boccaccio was close to the action. The new regime, which upheld the practice of excluding the most powerful aristocrats (magnates) from office, broadened its representative character by admitting shopkeepers and artisans from the lower guilds into its government. Butchers, swordmakers and wine merchants were to be elected with greater frequency to the Signoria than were members of leading patrician families such as the Albizzi, Strozzi and Medici. This extraordinary practice of restricting the role of the nobility in public life, which dated from 1293, was prompted by the endless factional violence between rival groupings: the struggle between (pro-papal) Guelfs and (pro-imperial) Ghibellines was continued by Black Guelfs and White Guelfs; many noble families, unable to forget their feudal origins, continued to exercise a private *vendetta* style of justice and to live as if outside or above the law. This Florentine policy of restricting the powers of nobles caused some difficulties in trade and diplomatic dealings. Northern Europeans, in particular, were used to working from a time-honoured equation between social identity and moral character: nobles behaved nobly, and *villeins* villainously. Writers such as Boccaccio played a vital role for Florence in suggesting how new forms of moral excellence might be exemplified by characters of humble or intermediate social status.

The greater guilds which controlled the most important Florentine industries did not think that the principle of *libertas* should include the lower classes, and the shopkeepers and artisans of the lower guilds were keen to accentuate their own privileged status by keeping the lower classes out of office. Cloth workers were not even allowed to form their own guild. This meant that the proletariat felt no particular loyalty to the regime, which was finally brought down by a revolt of unemployed wool-workers in 1378 (just three years before the English Peasants' Revolt). Those who held any kind of executive, legislative or judicial office in Florence served for a very short fixed term: the priors of the Signoria served for just two months; members of the Twelve and the Sixteen, the colleges which advised them, were in office for three and four months respectively. Citizens were not trusted with the administration and enforcement of justice: outsiders were hired on short, fixed-term contracts to serve as *podestà* (chief administrator) and *capitano del popolo* (commander of the militia). Their tasks were not easy since Florence was a perennially unruly and often violent city. Things were made more difficult by the Parte Guelfa, a society of ultra-conservative pro-papal nobles which forced its political enemies out of civic life by branding them as Ghibellines, disloyal to the Holy Roman Church. (There were as many Ghibellines in Florence in the 1340s as there were communists in Dallas in the 1950s.) Through this purely negative political tactic of *ammonizione*, which has much in common with McCarthyism, many magnates were able to exert some influence on the civic life from which they were formerly excluded.

Florentines were undoubtedly proud of their Republican system of government and were anxious to save it from sliding into despotism, the fate of most Republics in Trecento Italy. But there was no denying the fragility of Florentine political structures, which (through short-term contracts and the employment of outsiders for law enforcement) expressed distrust of rather than confidence in the initiatives of any single individual or group. To conceal such fragmentation and to present the outside world with a unified political front the Florentines developed what we would now call a civic ideology. Such ideology, much of it generated in response to the despotic and expansionist Visconti, who threatened Tuscany from the north, celebrated the transcendent power of Florentine *libertas* and deplored the barbarities of despotism. Boccaccio's *Decameron*, which shows how the communal, self-governing instincts of Florentine polity are kept alive through a period of social collapse, makes a significant and timely contribution to this civic ideology.

It was sadly ironical (an irony probably apparent to the Florentines themselves) that Florence's commitment to communal values may have made its experience of the Black Death all the more devastating. During the spring and summer of 1347 thousands of weak and hungry peasants fled from famine in the *contado* or countryside to seek food in Florence. The charitable company of Or San Michele, located at one of the city's busiest piazzas, ran its ovens day and night in a mighty attempt to save them from starvation. But the presence of so many homeless and debilitated people in the city meant, of course, that the ensuing plague was able to spread all the more rapidly. Those who stuck to their pastoral or communal tasks most loyally were most likely to die:

the Dominican monastery of Santa Maria Novella, attached to the church in which Boccaccio's *brigata* first assembles, lost 83 of its 130 friars; Boccaccio's father, who was an officer of the commune responsible for supervising rationing and hygiene, also died. Municipal authorities in Milan, the chief city of the Visconti despots, were less compassionate: any house containing a plague victim was bricked up, leaving the living to die with the dead. This brutal policy was successful: Milan suffered the lowest mortality rate of any city in Italy and (with Liège) in western Europe.

Boccaccio spent some time in Romagna during the years immediately preceding the plague, and it is not known exactly when he recrossed the Apennines and returned to Florence. But as a survivor of the plague and a fully enfranchised head of household (participation in political life was restricted to males over thirty), Boccaccio immediately took a full part in Florentine political life. When Florence went to war with the Visconti in 1351 he was sent on a series of important diplomatic missions; in 1354 he was Florentine ambassador to Pope Innocent VI at Avignon. It is important to emphasize that the writing of the *Decameron* complements rather than competes with Boccaccio's dedication to the Florentine body politic. The hygienic and therapeutic powers of literature in alleviating the pains and depressions of adversity were (as Glending Olson has shown) widely recognized by medical authorities in the Middle Ages. And the impulse to narrate the Florentine response to moments of danger or catastrophe was shared by a strong, well-established tradition of historiographical prose, written by men who shared Boccaccio's mercantile origins. The most famous of them was Giovanni Villani; Boccaccio, it seems, had privileged access to Giovanni's work before it entered general circulation.

Giovanni Villani's *Cronica* begins with the creation of the world and ends with the words: 'And the plague lasted until   '. Giovanni never filled in the blank because he did not survive 1348; his brother Matteo, however, continued his work. Giovanni was a deeply pious man who was concerned to square historical events (floods, comets, earthquakes and plagues as well as news of events – *novelle* – from home and abroad) with the workings of God. In Matteo and his successors, this impulse slackens as the Florentine commune itself (rather than the Almighty) becomes the real hero of history. The *Decameron* occupies, or shares, a crucial, transitional moment in this historiographical tradition, this sequence of attempts to explain the meaning of history in Italian prose for an audience of Florentines.

Chapter 2

The *Decameron*

Title and preface

The *Decameron* opens with a short rubric or explanatory heading in which it declares its own name and its surname or alternative title ('Prencipe Galeotto'). It then analyses its own contents with mathematical precision: one hundred tales told in ten days by seven young women and three young men. Although this and all later rubrics speak in an impersonal third person, we know (from the autograph manuscript Hamilton 90 in the Berlin Staatsbibliothek) that they were written by Boccaccio himself. The use of those rubrics, which employ an analytic vocabulary drawn from scholastic sources, suggests that Boccaccio (who names himself only as *l'autore*, the author) wishes his readers to consider the *Decameron* as a literary *opus*, not just as a collection of stories. Many medieval authors (Chaucer, for example) choose to address the reader directly with an authorial 'I' when speaking of the content and organization of the work in progress. By transferring most of this to third-person rubrics, Boccaccio assumes a more detached authorial positioning (typical, in some respects, of a historical chronicler). He addresses the reader directly at the beginning and end of his *opus*, and at the beginning of the fourth day, but otherwise remains largely concealed beneath the narrative surface.

It is strange that Boccaccio should bring the *Decameron* before us as a work with two names, even stranger that these names should compete with rather than gloss or complement one another. The name 'Decameron' recalls the familiar (to a medieval audience) title *Hexaemeron*, a name given to certain patristic treatises on God's six days of work in Genesis: the number ten (*deca*) is St Bonaventure's *numerus perfec-*

tissimus; the hundred *novelle* matched the hundred cantos of Dante's *Commedia*. But the name 'Prencipe Galeotto' (Prince Galahalt) alludes to the king (originally an enemy of King Arthur) who arranged for Queen Guinivere to meet Lancelot and then urged her to kiss him. This kiss, the first sign that the unity of the Round Table will be broken, is recalled or reenacted in *Inferno* V, where Paolo and Francesca are led to embrace by their reading (some say misreading) of the Guinivere and Lancelot story. Francesca, condemned to be blown and buffeted by a wind that externalizes her own passion, equates the author with his book and curses them both: 'Galeotto fu il libro e chi lo scrisse' (V, 137: 'Galeotto was the book and he who wrote it'). This, then, is the name Boccaccio chooses for his own work and (by Francesca's logic) for himself: he is a Galahalt, a Pandarus (these two names are closely associated as go-betweens in unhappy love affairs) bringing his readers to his text. This readership is soon to be defined and addressed as a female one; Boccaccio's relationship to women, and to women readers, is problematical right from the start.

The brief *proemio* offers an important opportunity to assess this Boccaccian first-person narrator before he disappears into his story-telling. The first four periods of the opening paragraph are exceptionally lengthy and eventful; here is the first:

Umana cosa è aver compassione degli afflitti: e come che a ciascuna persona stea bene, a coloro è massimamente richiesto li quali già hanno di conforto avuto mestiere e hannol trovato in alcuni; fra' quali, se alcuno mai n'ebbe bisogno o gli fu caro o già ne ricevette piacere, io sono uno di quegli.

To take pity on people in distress is a human quality which every man and woman should possess, but it is especially requisite in those who have once needed comfort, and found it in others. I number myself as one of these, because if ever anyone required or appreciated comfort, or indeed derived pleasure therefrom, I was that person.   (p. 45)

The *proemio* opens by speaking of the distinctively human quality of compassion, but adheres to an anonymous third-person singular ('Umana cosa è') until the speaker suddenly individuates himself as one among many who have actually experienced compassion at a moment of need: 'io sono uno di quegli' ('I am one of them'). This sudden emergence of the first-person subject, who at once establishes an individual and communal identity, is made the more dramatic by the clinching rhythm of a specific accentual pattern: 'úno di quégli'. This particular pattern (⌣ - - - ⌣ -), known as *cursus planus*, is one of the three most common patterns of the *cursus*, the system of rhythmical cadences employed in medieval *ars dictaminis*, the art of letter writing. The lines quoted above contain no fewer than seven instances of *cursus planus*, a much higher density than we will find in the *novelle* to come; their rhetoric is more colloquial, less highly wrought. Medieval authors often choose to establish their literary credentials by opening with an exceptionally complex and sophisticated period: the opening sentence of *The Canterbury Tales*, for example, does not discover its main verb until line fourteen ('thanne longen folk. . .'). Boccaccio, like Chaucer, makes it clear from the start that although the narrator may be a failure or has-been in love, he is no fool with a pen.

In his second paragraph Boccaccio tells how his experience of love has made him a subject fit for compassion. The subject of love immediately embroils us in questions of social degree, what we would now call class: Boccaccio is a man of 'humble condition' ('bassa condizione') who has loved a woman high above his station. This won him the admiration of many people, since such love has ennobling effects on the lover; at the same time it proves difficult to endure. All this is consistent with what the most famous medieval handbook has to say on the subject, the *De arte honeste amandi* of Andreas Capellanus. Andreas devotes a good deal of space to a series of dialogues between lovers of unequal social status: the second of these (in which a man of the middle class speaks with a woman of the nobility) most closely resembles Boccaccio's predicament. The opening words of Andreas's first chapter, in which he tells us 'what love is', also help us understand why lovers merit our compassion: 'love is a certain inborn suffering derived from the sight of and excessive meditation upon the beauty of the opposite sex' (Parry, p. 28). Love here resembles a disease: love sickness, or *amor hereos*, was analysed and treated as a disease by medieval medical authorities. The kind of 'immoderate passion' Boccaccio suffered could have immensely destructive effects, both on the patient (internally) and on society (externally): medieval political theory defined the tyrant as one who acts on his feelings rather than seeking the good of society, the *bonum commune*. The regulation of personal appetites (Boccaccio speaks of his 'poco regolato appetito') was a matter in which ethics shaded into politics. This theme is explored in detail on the tenth day.

In his third period, an exceptionally short one, Boccaccio finds relief from the miseries of private anguish in the pleasurable conversation ('i piacevoli ragionamenti') and the admirable support of friends. This saves him from a self-destructive death in much the same way as it saves Dante at a crucial moment of the *Vita nuova* (chapter XVIII). The whole *Decameron* reenacts this turn to the social and re-affirms its efficacy and wisdom.

The fourth and final period of this opening paragraph brings us to the narrator's present state of mind by speaking of the end of love. This is surprising, since we are more used to hearing of the *beginning* of love at the beginning of a literary text: the God of Love (in the *Filostrato*, and in *Troilus and Criseyde* after it) draws back his bow, and the lover-hero is smitten. Here, by contrast, God (He who is infinite, 'infinito') decides that Boccaccio's love should diminish by process of time ('in processo di tempo'). This reference to time, the dimension which sustains the *Decameron*'s narration, reminds us that the remedy for plague and the cure for love are one and the same: time must pass. (It is worth noting that the term 'plague' was derived from the Latin *plaga*, meaning a violent blow: the love-struck and the plague-struck were similarly afflicted by terrible forces beyond their control.) Once love (and plague) have been outlasted, they survive only in the memory as a feeling that may be drawn into conscious recollection. Boccaccio's epistemology here is reminiscent of Dante's: present feelings offer the clue or index for the authenticity of past experiences (such as a journey through the afterlife) that the intellect may now struggle to recapture and put into words.

Perhaps the most significant absence we note in this opening paragraph is any sense of the individuality of the woman Boccaccio loved: she is mentioned just once, in generic terms ('della donna amata', 3). The attitude to women developed in Boccaccio's *proemio* is problematic and ultimately contradictory. By choosing to write in Italian Boccaccio commits himself to the supposition that he is writing primarily for women, since in the proto-humanist circles of Trecento Italy learned authors were men who wrote for other men in Latin. Petrarch, in writing to Boccaccio in 1373, assumes that the *Decameron* cannot merit his serious attention because it is written in 'our mother tongue' (*Seniles XVII, 3*). In his *proemio*, then, Boccaccio presents his vernacular writing as a kind of *post facto Frauendienst* which repays a debt of gratitude to women for past kindness. Boccaccio's sympathy for women, or the simple fact of his perceiving how young women lead their lives, is impressive: 'they are forced to follow the whims, fancies and dictates of their fathers, mothers, brothers and husbands, so that they spend most of their time cooped up within the narrow confines of their rooms' (10; p. 46). Men, by comparison, 'can always walk abroad, see and hear many things, go fowling, hunting, fishing, riding and gambling, or attend to their business affairs' (12; p. 47). But Boccaccio's gift of writing, ironically, is not going to get women out of the house: except imaginatively, through the power of his text. The women of the *Decameron*'s *brigata* do leave their rooms and organize an alternative society. But this happens during the plague, a time when the usual rules and mores of society are held in suspension.

First day (introduction)

The *Decameron*'s introduction may be considered in two parts: the description of the plague (sections 2–48 of the

Italian: McWilliam, pp. 49–58) and the mise-en-scène of the storytelling framework (49–115; pp. 58–68). This division is not marked in the manuscripts but it is, I shall suggest, observed by both the form and content of Boccaccio's prose.

The plague

In his first paragraph Boccaccio assures his immediate readership, now established as a female one, that his description of the plague is a 'brief unpleasantness' that will soon be followed by 'sweetness and pleasure'. This promise is borne out by the introduction itself, which moves us from the misery and grotesquerie of a diseased and disorderly city to the delightful company of young, noble and beautiful people gathered in a country garden. Such a dramatic contrast is a familiar feature of contemporary Italian frescoes, the Triumph of Death cycle at Pisa being perhaps the most famous example. However, by moving *from* death and decay *to* youthful merrymaking, Boccaccio throws the narrative sequence of the moralizing fresco into reverse.

Having reestablished the kind of intimate contact with a female readership we might associate with a courtly lyricist, Boccaccio at once (in his second paragraph) shifts perspective dramatically and speaks like a historiographer. Like Villani before him, Boccaccio situates recent events within the greater span of Christian time: the pestilence hits Florence one thousand, three hundred and forty-eight years after the Incarnation of Christ (10; p. 50). In describing the catastrophic flood of 1333, which had seen Florentines hopping across the rooftops as the city went under water, Villani had recorded alternative explanations for this disaster: perhaps God was punishing Florence for its great and manifold sins; or perhaps it just rained too much. Boccaccio follows Villani in offering both natural and supernatural explanations for the onset of catastrophe. But rather than choose between them he observes the spread of the plague from east to west, evoking a huge spatial dimension that complements the large temporal span he began with. This allows him to observe the behaviour of Florentines in Florence in 1348 with the detachment of a historian or (to risk an anachronism) an anthropologist.

Boccaccio is a detached observer, but not an indifferent one: he speaks as a survivor of plague (and survivor of love) who records the desperate strategies of those trapped in the wrong place at the wrong time. History acquires pathos, as Boccaccio contemplates it, by virtue of this difference between the objective knowledge and relative security of *now* and the claustrophobic subjectivity of *then*, the moment of the plague. It is only through the power of such imaginative retrospection that the plague becomes fully visible or intelligible: those trapped within the plague-stricken city find the vision of mortality that confronts them so overpowering that, for the most part, they close their minds to it (41; p. 56).

The citizens of Florence, secure within their city walls, like to think of Florentine society as a self-sufficient organic unity. Before and after plague, the integrity and cohesiveness of the social body is guaranteed and regulated by time-honoured customs ('Era usanza, sì come ancora oggi veggiamo usare', 32; p. 54). But during the plague itself such continuity is disrupted, and strange new words are heard which attest to the sickness of both the personal body and the body politic. Men and women discover strange, egg-shaped swellings under their armpits which the populace call *gavoccioli* (section 10; p. 50). The *gavocciolo* is the first sign of death; bodies pile up, and a new class of entrepreneurs called *becchini* springs up from the lower orders to clear the traffic (35; p. 55). But perhaps the most noteworthy sign of change in the disease-ridden city is a new attitude towards women. In the *proemio*, we have noted, women spend most of their time cooped up in their rooms, 'forced to follow the whims, fancies and dictates of their fathers, mothers, brothers and husbands' (10; p. 46). But during the plague everyone abandons everyone else (27; p. 54) and the structures which distinguish private from public space simply collapse. Woman who grow sick in their rooms, abandoned by maidservants and relatives, are forced to expose or open ('aprire', 29) their bodies to the world, specifically to any male servants who can be retained for wages. 'And this', Boccaccio adds, 'explains why those women who recovered were possibly less chaste in the period that followed' (29; p. 54).

This gratuitous little remark reveals the misogynistic flip-side of Boccaccio's devotion to women. There is no doubting the sincerity of his devotion: but its very idealizing intensity means that moments of disillusion and disappointment will send him to the opposite end of the woman-as-saint-or-sinner paradigm. Boccaccio (and medieval men in general) attributes such volatility to women themselves: when he speaks of 'vaghe donne' (*proemio* 9; p. 46) he is thinking not only of the adjective *vaga* (charming, gracious) but also of its etymological roots in the verb *vagare* (to wander, as in our term 'vagrant'). 'We women,' one of his *brigata* ladies declares, 'are fickle [mobili], quarrelsome, suspicious, cowardly, and easily frightened' (introduction, 75; p. 62). In Boccaccio's case it is not difficult to diagnose this malady of female instability as masculine projection on an epic scale. Boccaccio himself, given the ironic nickname of 'John the Tranquil' by one of his male friends, was exceptionally *mobile* in moving between the ideal of chastity and the practice of sexual relations: although he tried to live as a celibate (and may have become a priest in later years) he fathered quite a number of illegitimate children. Five of these who died in infancy show up to claim paternity in his dream poem *Olympia*.

One of the traditional roles accorded to women, Boccaccio notes, is their habit of gathering around a dead or dying man and comforting him with prayers (32–4; pp. 54–5). But during the plague few women show up, and those that do neglect their prayers and treat the moment of death as 'the signal for laughter and witticisms and general jollification' (34; p. 55). Such female festivity ('festeggiar'), which supplants traditional 'feminine concern for the salvation of the souls of the dead', itself signals a turn in Boccaccio's narration from the realistic to the surreal and (ultimately) the grotesque. Bodies left outside doorways are piled onto planks and carried off in search of a priest. Long trains of corpses are formed en route to the graveyard. Huge trenches are dug and the dead are 'stowed tier upon tier like ships' cargo' (42; p. 57). The churchyard thus becomes a ship of death, or a ship of fools, and the dead are shown no more respect 'than would nowadays be shown towards dead goats' (41; p. 56). This casual reference to goats reminds us, of course, that the grotesqueries of this scene are darkened by a subliminal awareness of Christian (sheep and goats) eschatology. We might look to Bosch for visual equivalents, although (Millard Meiss has argued) Florentine painting after the Black Death offers many appropriate images of its own.

Before winding up his account of the plague Boccaccio takes a brief look at conditions in the surrounding country-side or *contado* (43–6; p. 57). He does not stay long outside the city walls since, for Florentines, the *contado* holds little intrinsic interest; political life begins and ends (and takes its name) from the *polis*, or city-state. In proposing the move to the *contado*, Pampinea is mindful of the attractions of hills, trees, birdsong and country air, but chiefly as an antidote to the current desolation of the city. Besides, she suggests, there are fewer dead bodies per square foot in the countryside; farmworkers die discreetly, in far-flung farm-houses (68; p. 61). There is no suggestion that the countryside possesses any independent power or mystique in the *Decameron*; it represents a convenient space for Florentines to colonize by imposing their own elegant and urbane procedures.

Returning somewhat peremptorily to the city ('lasciando star il contado', 47), Boccaccio confronts us once again with the bare statistics of disaster: who died when, and in what numbers. But halfway through this last paragraph on the plague he switches abruptly from a historiographical to a lyrical mode, ringing changes on the *ubi sunt* ('where are they now?') *topos*. Even at the high point of rhetorical *exclamatio*, we should notice, Boccaccio's imagination is stirred by prac-tical details: how many 'vast estates' and 'notable fortunes' are 'left without a rightful successor!' (48; p. 58). The outpouring of rhetorical energy here allows some egress for the difficult emotions accumulated through the preceding paragraphs. At the same time it seals off the general description of the plague through a decisive stylistic closure that features three sets of noun triplets ('Galen, Hippocrates and Aesculapius', etc.) and an exceptionally heavy incidence of *cursus* rhythms. And yet although this closure is *stylistically* final, and the paragraph ends with the finality of death, there is something characteristically resilient, almost cheerful, about Boccaccio's vision of breakfast with relatives in this world and supper with ancestors in the next (48; p. 58).

The mise-en-scène

In assembling his ten young storytellers Boccaccio makes a rapid descent from the grand sweep of historiographical time to the relative precision of 'one Tuesday morning' (49; p. 58). And yet having been more specific than before he immediately becomes more vague by adding a parenthetic qualification: '(or so I was told by a person whose word can be trusted)'. Such problematizing of the historical basis of the narrative might be taken to signal a transition to a purely fictional world. And yet it is worth noting that the preceding plague description, so often anthologized as a historical document produced by an eye-witness, is itself modelled after a literary source, namely the account of the plague during the reign of Justinian in the *Historia Langobardorum* of Paulus Diaconus (died c. 799). This is not to say that Boccaccio is a liar and a fraud. We must recognize that the Middle Ages had its own distinctive ideas about what makes a text authentic and meaningful: there are more important things in life than empirical observation. In recording the capture of a dolphin in the Thames in 1391 the chronicler Thomas Walsingham described its habits not from first-hand observation but from the appropriate page of Pliny's *Natural History*. The meaning of this dolphin only became clear in 1392 when Walsingham (a Benedictine monk) recognized it as an omen of political trouble between Richard II and the Londoners. Boccaccio does not share Walsingham's straightforward theocentric reading of history, but he is closer to Walsingham than he is to us.

Boccaccio brings us quickly to a circle of women reciting their prayers in the church of Santa Maria Novella. This is the kind of group that Boccaccio has already associated with a dead man's bedside: we do not immediately perceive them as a *brigata* of storytellers. They do not recognize themselves, initially, as a group that has the right to act on their own initiative in their own interest; Pampinea (the eldest of the seven) must speak at some length before arriving at the overwhelming questions: 'What are we doing here? What are we waiting for? What are we dreaming about?' (63; p. 60). The chief obstacle confronting them is, of course, the founding myth of gender relations in the west: that woman took the initiative in Eden and got us thrown out of the garden. This scenario is evoked, intertextually, even as Pampinea argues that the move to the countryside may be achieved 'without in any way overstepping the bounds of what is reasonable' (p. 61; 'senza trapassare in alcuno atto il segno della ragione', 65). This echoes Dante's Adam, who explains in *Paradiso* XXVI, 115–17 that Eden was lost not through the eating of the fruit *per se* but rather through crossing the boundary of obedience ('il trapassar del segno').

It is wholly predictable, then, that Pampinea's call to action should be countered by the familiar argument that woman cannot act alone since 'man is the head of woman' (76; p. 62). Fortunately, however, three suitable masculine heads arrive right on cue. These three are of the appropriate age and social class and are each related to one or other of the seven ladies. They are also in love with three of the ladies, which means that they are susceptible to female influence and control; their headship is nominal. The men play no part in planning the move to the countryside or in devising the machinery of the story-telling.

Various efforts have been made to explore the individual character and psychology of Boccaccio's storytellers. Their names offer points of departure: Elissa, for example, is an alternative name for Virgil's Dido, and Lauretta is a diminutive of Laura, Petrarch's beloved. The fact that Boccaccio gives his storytellers literary names (most of them drawn from his own earlier fictions) suggests, however, that they are to be seen precisely as *literary* figures rather than as real people in literary disguise. In any event, attempts at tracing the evolving characters of specific storytellers through the *Decameron* have met with very little success. It is clear that Boccaccio is interested in the workings of the group as a group rather than in its constituent individuals.

The group which is established under Pampinea's guidance is an ideal model of associative polity which is untroubled by traditional hierarchizing factors such as age, class, and gender. Authority is transferred on a daily basis (a short term of office even by Florentine standards) so that each person may experience 'the burden of responsibility and the pleasure of command associated with sovereign power' (96; p. 65). Perhaps the best visual equivalent here is Ambrogio Lorenzetti's representation of good government in the famous Sienese fresco, in which twenty-four citizens of exactly equal stature stand in a line to embody the Ciceronian ideal of *aequitas* (Skinner 1986, p. 34). Political realities were a little different, although all Florentine associations (from the Signoria to the humblest parish guild) did strive to observe this principle of equality *across* the group. But there were, of course, considerable distances between associative groupings at different social levels. This sense of *vertical* distance is represented in the *Decameron* through the space that separates the *brigata* of storytellers from the group of servants that attends them.

This group of four female and three male servants forms a sort of shadow-*brigata* that marks the limits of Florentine political ideology. Separated from the main *brigata* by a significant social distance, their group does not even enjoy an internal equality at its own social level: Pampinea assigns the women more menial tasks than the men and puts them under masculine authority (98–101; p. 66); there is no mention of authority here being shared or rotated. The ideal prescribed for this shadow-*brigata* is silence and invisibility; tables are found ready-laid and meals are served without a sound. The servants play very little part in the *Decameron*, although they do make a brief and noisy irruption into the beginning of the sixth day. This is allowed to run on for a while until it is brought abruptly, almost brutally, to an end. All this is very different from Chaucer's *Canterbury Tales*, which sees a great deal of conflict and contention between diverse social classes even though the initial narrative premise of a story-telling contest is soon forgotten. Pampinea makes it abundantly clear that storytelling in the *Decameron* is not to be seen as a competitive activity (111; p. 68). Competition (as in chess, for example) would disrupt the unanimity of the *brigata*. But this harmonious ideal requires not only isolation from the plague but also the exclusion of any antagonistic social force. So although the *brigata* is happy to hear stories of people of low degree outwitting their social superiors, or sleeping with them, there is no question of such activity escaping from the containing framework of the fiction.

As the setting-up of the storytelling machinery is completed and the first tale is called for, it might seem that the *brigata* is in perfect control of events. But a sense of historical uncertainty, of moment-to-moment contingency, remains with them throughout; they are, after all, hiding from the Black Death. It is worth recalling that Pampinea, in proposing the move to the countryside, reminded the young storytellers that they themselves are actors in a great historical plot whose end (*fine*, a scholastic term employed by medieval literary theorists) is not yet known:

In this way of life we shall continue until such time as we discover (provided we are spared from early death) the end [fine] decreed by Heaven for these terrible events.   (71; p. 62)

First day: the saint's life and the powers of language

On the first day (and on the ninth) no narrative theme is prescribed: storytellers are free to follow their own inclinations. Boccaccio's opening *novella* is astonishing by any standards, medieval or modern. In writing of a time of plague when thousands are dying daily, he chooses to open with a deathbed drama that forms the centrepiece of a historical, geographical and eschatological canvas of huge dimensions.

These dimensions become evident from the very first sentences of the storytelling proper, which quickly lays out a complex network of dependencies. We begin with Musciatto Franzesi, an Italian merchant who has grown wealthy and powerful through trading in France and is consequently recognized by the French court as 'a gentleman' (p. 69; more precisely as a knight, 'cavalier', 1, 7). Such recognition lays him under obligation and he is dispatched to Tuscany on business in the company of Carlo Senzaterra, brother of the French king; Carlo has himself been summoned by the Pope. Musciatto realizes that while he is caught up with affairs in Tuscany he will need somebody who is at once evil ('malvagio', 8) and trustworthy to recover some loans in Burgundy. This brings us to our protagonist, Ser Cepparello da Prato.

Boccaccio could certainly have brought us to Cepparello much faster: why all these preliminaries, which centre on a character (Musciatto) who will play no further part in the action? My suggestion is that before he lets Cepparello loose on the narrative, Boccaccio wishes to focus attention on the network of social, political, and economic relationships within which he operates. Musciatto is the middle-man in this arrangement: he is recognized as a knight by the French court, but to guarantee this honour he must continue to serve as a merchant and money-lender and for this he needs Cepparello. The Pope needs Carlo Senzaterra and Carlo needs Musciatto. Cepparello, then, operates at the bottom end of a chain of dependencies that connects money-lenders in Burgundy with the French royal court and the *pontifex maximus*.

It is worth noting that there was, in fact, a Musciatto Franzesi who did business in France. For Florentine historiographers, Musciatto (with his Brother Biccio) was the archetypal crooked operator: he induced the French king, Philip the Fair, to use counterfeit coinage and to fleece Italian merchants; Philip rewarded him with the title of *gentil-homme*. There was also a Cepparello da Prato who collected taxes for Philip the Fair and Pope Boniface VIII and spent some time in Burgundy. Cepparello and Musciatto did do business together; and Carlo Senzaterra (Charles Stateless, an ironic nickname alluded to by Dante in *Purgatorio* XX, 76) was summoned to Tuscany by Pope Boniface VIII in 1301. Charles was ostensibly briefed to keep the peace between the Black and White Guelfs in Florence, but the Pope's real purpose was to establish the pro-papal Blacks in power and hunt out the Whites. This strategy of betrayal (Dante compares Charles with Judas in *Purgatorio* XX, 73–4) was successfully executed and Dante was exiled with his fellow Whites. While the Cepparello story is plainly not gospel truth, then, it bristles with names, places, and historical events that were still potently evocative for Florentines in 1350. The ingenious complexity of its narrative framework bears some relation to a complex historical network of merchant capital, religious authority, and secular power.

At this point we should perhaps turn back to the long opening paragraph of this first *novella*. Readers tend to skip through this first paragraph in some haste, regarding it as no more than a piece of conventional piety: it was, after all, conventional (as Panfilo says) to begin a story by acknowledging 'Him that was maker of all things' (2; p. 68). But in this instance the acknowledgment goes on at quite exceptional length and so demands to be reckoned with. The following story, Boccaccio says, tells of one of God's 'marvellous works'; by hearing it we will strengthen our faith 'in Him as in something immutable' (2; p. 69). This, given the complex of intrigue and betrayal in which the story unfolds, seems most improbable: unless we can recognize that God operates not only above and beyond the vision of 'the human eye', but also beyond the institutional forms that purport to carry his revelation to the world. This is not a heretical position: indeed, a medieval Catholic would have thought it heretical to suggest that God was free to operate only in those ways that human language and religious institutions had prepared for him. Fourteenth-century nominalist theologians distinguished between God's *potentia ordinata*, his power of entering into historical covenants and agreements with us, and his *potentia absoluta*, his absolute freedom to act outside or beyond them. Boccaccio's *novella* celebrates this freedom and explores its consequences.

The religious institution that Boccaccio devotes most space to is that of intercession by the saints, those canonized middlemen who relay the prayers and petitions of the sinful to God. On bringing us to Cepparello, Boccaccio at once tells us of his life: 'Era questo Ciappelletto di questa vita' (10; p. 70). What follows is a perfect inversion of a favourite medieval genre, the saint's life: Ciappelletto (as he is now called) prides himself on his wickedness and strives mightily ('forte vi studiava', 12) to be perfect in it. Such constancy in evil makes him predictable, even reliable, and hence indispensable to Musciatto. Ciappelletto turns the moral world upside down, robbing and stealing 'as conscientiously as if he were a saintly man making an offering' (14; p. 71). His appetites are in all respects *contrario*: he is as fond of women 'as dogs are fond of a good stout stick' (meaning not at all: dogs run from a beating); he finds his pleasure in 'their opposite ('del contrario', meaning homosexuality). Boccaccio lets Ciappelletto's *vita* run on for quite some time before ending abruptly: 'But why do I lavish so many words upon him? He was perhaps the worst man ever born' (15; p. 71).

Panfilo's question is worth pondering: why does he commit himself to so many words ('mi distendo io in tante parole') in describing Ciappelletto? Because, of course, such description is pleasurable. Some of this comes over in translation, although the great rolling vowels and strong, stressed consonants of the long Italian words (or clusters of words elided) need to be read aloud if we are to taste the full pleasure of moral censoriousness: 'Bestemmiatore di Dio e de' Santi era grandissimo. . .' (13; p. 71). But the vigour of such condemnation is only a flimsy cover for the pleasure we take in the punctilious intensity and sheer vibrant energy of Ciappelletto himself. And when both narrator and reader become fascinated by that which they are expected to condemn we have a more complex moral dilemma. Dante experiences this deep down in the Inferno when he becomes so engrossed in a slanging match between Master Adam (who counterfeited coin) and Sinon (who betrayed Troy) that Virgil is obliged to step in and break the spell (XXX, 49–148). Virgil ends this canto by warning that 'the wish to hear of such [base] things is a base wish'. The point was entirely wasted on Dante's early commentators, who go to great and exuberant lengths in recording the various scams and con-tricks Dante's *dannati* are credited with. The *Decameron* itself fairly swarms with the kind of perverted energies that are found damnable in Dis, Dante's infernal city. What, then, are the consequences or implications of making such energies a source of narrative entertainment? Boccaccio does not appear to address this question, although we should recall that the *Decameron* is surnamed 'Prince Galahalt', the go-between text that can lead to ruin. Boccaccio's ladies commend the whole of Panfilo's story and laugh at parts of it (I, 2, 2; p. 82). The trick, it seems, is to laugh only at the right places. Such precarious positioning on the moral responsibilities of authors and readers is not untypical of medieval vernacular texts.

Once Musciatto has spoken to Ciappelletto the plot moves swiftly into gear again: Ciappelletto travels to Burgundy, lodges with two Florentine money-lenders and sets about the business of recovering loans. Just as abruptly, this forward movement stops: Ciappelletto gets sick and rapidly declines, like one who is suffering the sickness of death ('il male della morte', 21; p. 72). It is at this liminal point, this *limen* or threshold between life and death, that Ciappelletto conceives of his plan for a spectacular confession, his first and last.

The dialogue between the kindly old confessor (whom Ciappelletto addresses with a respectful 'voi') and the fraudulent penitent (addressed with a familiar 'tu') offers Boccaccio the perfect opportunity to display the imaginative virtuosity of 'the worst man who ever lived'. As we run through the sins of passion (lust, gluttony, avarice, anger), the 'holy friar' (Boccaccio persists in calling him 'santo') seems little more than a stereotypical dupe, the good and credulous man of religion. Indeed, he is so comprehensively deceived that he is encouraged to make confessions of his own: Ciappelletto should not worry about spitting in church, for example, because 'we members of religious orders spit there continually' (63; p. 77). But as the confession progresses, and Ciappelletto's performance becomes ever more dramatic, the 'holy friar' begins to develop a vision of his own that challenges the audacity and epic scale of Ciappelletto's imaginings: however great or abundant the sin, on whatever time-scale, nothing can defeat the benignity and compassion of God (68, 72; p. 78). The friar believes, in his verbal duelling with Ciappelletto, that the greatest threat to Ciappelletto's salvation is despair. And he is absolutely right, although he has no idea that Ciappelletto has already despaired and is speaking, as it were, from the far side: their progress through the confessional manual matches the downward itinerary of Dante's Hell, a journey that Ciappelletto apparently believes he is certain to make. The comic genius of Ciappelletto's mock-confessing works against a hard edge of religious dread that makes it all the more compelling. The Florentine money-lenders who overhear it in secret 'nearly exploded with mirth', and yet are led to echo words of wonder and astonishment first evinced by the miracles of Christ: 'What manner of man is this. . .?' (78–9; p. 79: Matthew 8, 27).

Ciappelletto dies, and the 'holy friar' expresses the hope that God will work many miracles through him. His body is carried in procession by the whole town from the house of the money-lenders to the church of the friars. The 'santo frate' climbs into his pulpit and begins to fashion a new set-piece narrative: Ciappelletto's confession is transformed into a saint's life. Through the power of such narrativizing Ciappelletto's body becomes an icon and a source of relics; people who manage to rip a shred from his clothing feel transported to 'Paradise itself' (86; p. 80). The fame of his saintliness spreads; the cult of Saint Ciappelletto grows; miracles are reported.

Saints were big business in the Middle Ages. When a poten-
tial saint lay dying, an armed guard was often mounted to
dissuade anyone from snapping off a finger once *rigor mortis*
set in. A local saint could do a great deal for the local
economy: pilgrims flocked in, relics were sold, donations
made. When Florentines wished to control or punish small
towns in their *contado*, they would confiscate the relics of
local saints and transfer them to Florence, thereby robbing
the countryside of its localized charisma and bolstering their
own centralized power. Ciappelletto's confession, then,
might be read as a final pledge of loyalty to the religious and
commercial eco-system that sustained him in life, the network
of dependencies sketched out at the *novella*'s beginning. He
saves the Florentine money-lenders from the mob and his own
body from being flung into the ditch outside the city wall
(25–6; p. 72), the fate reserved for those who die through
suicide or as usurers, excommunicates or heretics. He supplies
fresh spiritual prestige to the friary, civic unity to the town,
and religious capital to the papacy which regulates canoniza-
tions. All this, of course, stands in dubious relationship to
'the name of Him with whom we began our storytelling' (p.
81).

The *Decameron*'s next two tales further this exploration of
the problematical or enigmatic relationship of transcendent
truths to the religious forms that profess to embody them. In
I, 2 a Jewish merchant visits Rome and is convinced by the
utter depravity and corruption of the clergy that Christianity
must be true: how else, without divine inspiration, could it
continue to prosper and flourish? In I, 3 another Jew finds
a story to tell that saves him from having to choose between
Jewish, Muslim, and Christian accounts of revelation.
Dioneo, in the fourth *novella*, relieves us from large
theological questions by concentrating on more frivolous and
parochial affairs. He remains within a religious ambit (hanky-
panky in a monastery near Florence), but finds real continuity
with the preceding *novella* by concentrating on the social
efficacy of language: the art of finding the right words at
the right time. Such concern with the powers and pitfalls of

language is fundamental not only to this *giornata* but also to the entire *Decameron*.

The problem or paradox of seeking to express transcendent truths in human language is fully acknowledged by Dante in the *Commedia*'s recollection of the spiritual beyond. But even in the human world, the referential powers of language are often found to be insecure: this is imaged early on in the *Decameron* through the etymological confusions surrounding Cepparello's name as it passes from Italian to French (I, 1, 9; p. 70). And yet, whatever its inadequacies, language is the medium that makes and breaks the negotiations and understandings that structure and sustain life in the social world. Sometimes, as in I, 8 and I, 9, a situation can be saved (and an individual morally transformed) by a single word or phrase. At others, the wrong word can lead to ruin. In I, 6 a prosperous Florentine delivers himself into the hands of a Franciscan inquisitor with a single idle boast: his wine is so good 'that Christ himself would have drunk it' (5; p. 96). These errant words transform him from law-abiding citizen to heretic and commit him to further bizarre changes: he must become a doctor to the friars (massaging them with the ointment of money); he must play the part of a penitent and wear a cross 'which made him look as if he were about to set off on a Crusade' (10; p. 97). Finally he manages to play the part of scriptural exegete (the friar's own role) and so expose the friar's hypocrisy. And so he returns to his original point of departure through language, the means through which he first forfeited his identity as 'a law-abiding citizen'.

The judicious exercise of language was of exceptional importance to fourteenth-century Florence. At Milan and other cities under despotic rule the art of public debate declined in the Trecento since, under the despot, no debate was thought necessary. Florence, as its archives show, was an extraordinarily talkative city: the delicate mechanisms of its complex associative polity could only be regulated through the continuous exercise of language. Through his experience of Florentine public life (and his reading of Cicero and the medieval *ars dictaminis*), Boccaccio came to understand how language needed to change or adapt when addressing people of differing social degree in variable circumstances. Many readers treated *novella* collections like the *Novellino*, the *Decameron* and Sacchetti's *Trecentonovelle* as urban variants of the medieval courtesy book, texts from which they could learn strategies for acting and speaking in the public sphere. A typical example of tactful and fruitful criticism of a social superior is *Decameron* I, 7, where Bergamino works under the shield or *scudo* of a story to reprove the momentary meanness of a celebrated patron, Can Grande della Scala.

The critic Guido Almansi has insisted that the language of the *Decameron* turns in on itself: that the *Decameron* is 'a completely self-sufficient text', a book 'qui s'écrit' ('which writes itself') and 'which stands at a considerable distance from mimesis and real life representation' (pp. 4, 5). Such a severely formalist reading, developed out of Philippe Sollers, can only be sustained by isolating the *Decameron* from the city-state culture within which it was written and of which it forms part. Although Boccaccio's *novelle* occasionally feature exotic or distant locales, the powers of language they exemplify are never far removed from those that govern the historical world: in both worlds words can make a saint, ruin and rehabilitate a citizen, offer a life-line of escape from tight corners and enable people of differing religious persuasion or social degree to meet, momentarily, on common territory. Almansi (in 1975) thought of the *Decameron* as 'the ideal text for the formalists to get their teeth into' (p. 4). But formalist readings such as Todorov's *Grammaire du Décaméron* now seem like misguided attempts to suck the historical life-blood from Boccaccio's book.

Second day: Fortune, female character and the impulse to trade

The second day tells of people who suffer various setbacks before finally achieving happiness. This movement from misery to joy, the movement of comedy, sees Boccaccio working with Fortune, one of the most familiar and yet most elusive of all medieval figures.

In Dante's *Commedia*, the pilgrim Dante has not descended far into the underworld before he feels compelled to ask Virgil the most basic question about Fortune: 'What is she?' (*Inferno* VII, 69: 'che è. . .?'). For Virgil, who views the world from a position outside of time, her identity is clear: Fortune is God's general minister and guide ('general ministra e duce', VII, 78), a heavenly intelligence who controls the shifting of prosperity and power from one people and one family bloodline to another. One such shift occurs in *Decameron* II, 8, which begins with the transfer of Roman imperial authority, the *translatio imperii*, from French to German hands. But the scope and expanse of Fortune's workings is most impressively suggested by the accumulative sequence of narratives in Boccaccio's second day. These ten *novelle* trace the movement of events through time across a vast geographical canvas.

The limits of the world traversed in the second day are marked by the British Isles in the north and by Araby (Arab territories) in the south. Both of these far-off regions seemed exotic, sometimes fantastic, to the medieval Italian. Britain (as represented by II, 3 and II, 8) forms part of Christendom but is governed by an archaic feudal polity. Such backwardness presents attractive opportunities to the astute Florentine who can get rich by mortgaging barons' castles (II, 3, 13; p. 129). Indeed, there seems to be no limit to what the Florentine entrepreneur might achieve: by the end of II, 3 Alessandro has been seduced by an abbot (a princess in disguise), reconciled Henry II with Henry III, been created Earl of Cornwall and, finally, made himself King of Scotland by right of conquest. Araby lies beyond Christendom and is hence a site for even more fantastic and exotic imaginative projections: at the end of II, 7 an Arab woman completes the journey to the man she was originally intended for, having travelled thousands of miles and made love to eight different men perhaps ten thousand times (II, 7, 121; p. 191). Araby may also afford a distanced, defamiliarizing perspective upon the sites and

convictions of Christendom: the same Arab woman speaks of
the Holy Sepulchre at Jerusalem as the place 'where the man
they look upon as God was buried after being killed by the
Jews' (II, 7, 112; p. 189).

The Arab world may also function as the extreme limit to
which a Christian protagonist must travel in order to discover
the truth of her own situation. In II, 9 Zinevra comes to Acre,
site of the trade fair that draws together Christians and
Saracens in large numbers (45; p. 215). Here she discovers the
objects stolen from her bedchamber that, she now realizes,
convinced her husband of her infidelity. This discovery,
which opens the way to her rehabilitation in Christendom, is
made possible by the world-wide circulation of commodities
that brings Arab and Christian together. Trade suddenly
rivals Fortune as the instrument of God's *arbitrium*. Such
romancing of the market economy reminds us that the banking and mercantile company to which Boccaccio was once
apprenticed spanned the whole world of the second day: the
Bardi had warehouses and offices in ten Italian cities as well
as in Avignon, Barcelona, Bruges, Cyprus, Constantinople,
Jerusalem, London, Majorca, Marseilles, Paris, Rhodes,
Seville, and Tunis.

Several second day *novelle* explore the workings of Fortune
as *aventure*, the concept governing the adventures of traditional romance. These longer, more luxuriant narratives
achieve effects of pathos by isolating a single, vulnerable
individual beneath a mighty framework of historical events.
Such effects are realized not through lyric or lament but
through *gesta*, a sequence of events: the most memorable example is perhaps that of Madonna Beritola, who loses her two
sons and then suckles two newly born roebucks on a remote
island (II, 6, 15–26; pp. 157–9). In these romance-style narratives the lover is typically convinced that his love transcends
the workings of Fortune: 'I loved your daughter, I love her
still, and I shall always love her' (II, 6, 54; p. 163). But
although the lover's feelings might defy the passage of time,
his body cannot: Boccaccio always takes pains to emphasise
how the bodies of exiles and unrequited lovers suffer and

decline. The body cannot recover until some event in the greater historical world (in II, 6 the conquest of Sicily by Peter of Aragon) unites or reconciles it with its object of desire.

When the movement of historical events secures the well-being of the individual, it is easy to discern the workings of God: 'He alone, out of His loving kindness' (we are told in II, 8) 'made possible the train of events which followed, in order to prevent this nobly-born maiden from falling into the hands of a commoner' (39; p. 197). It is obvious that God shares the narrator's notions of social decorum; and, of course, that He is masculine. When things work out well, as they do in II, 2, it is assumed that 'God and St Julian' have been pulling the strings (42; p. 126). When things go wrong, God changes His gender. Or rather, there is no talk of God directing events, only of Fortuna (a feminine noun) mishandling them. Fortune, like woman, is an enigma: 'the more one discusses her actions, the more remains to be said'; she 'arranges and rearranges [events] after her own inscrutable fashion (occulto giudicio), constantly moving them now in one direction, now in another, then back again, without following any discernible plan' (II, 3, 4; p. 127). Fortune is a seductress ('our mental faculties . . . are easily lulled to sleep by her blandishments'); men will be forewarned, or amused, by hearing 'an account of her eccentricities' (II, 6, 3; p. 155).

The name of Fortune, it seems, is invoked when the clear logic of God's workings in history becomes occluded, 'occulto'. At such moments (Virgil explains to Dante in *Inferno* VII) men habitually revile Fortune when they should praise her and recognize the limits of their own understanding (91–3). But although men cannot reproach the otherness of God, they can revile the otherness of woman and so gain some emotional relief from the fears and pressures of living in an unfolding historical present. For every statement about Fortune recycles and confirms basic assumptions about the difference between genders. Man, 'the most noble of God's mortal creatures', exemplifies stability, 'fermezza'. Women, created second to men, are fickle: 'le femine sono più mobili' (II, 9, 15; p. 209).

These last commonplaces sit oddly with the *novella* they introduce, since in II, 9 it is Bernabò, the merchant-husband, whose emotions are recklessly 'mobili': in a fit of passion, he wagers on the constancy of his wife's affections at odds of 5 to 1. Similarly, in II, 7 it is the restlessness of masculine desire that circulates a passive, voiceless woman around the world's sea-lanes: and yet the moralizing masculine storyteller sets out to castigate the restlessness of female desire (women should not wish to be more beautiful than Nature made them). Since Fortune is female, women are the primary targets for such moralization, for the injunction 'to resign ourselves to the acquisition and possession of whatever has been granted us by the One Who alone knows what we need and has the power to provide it for us' (II, 7, 6; p. 170). But the chief threat to such religious resignation lies not in the female character but in the impulse to trade that stirs so mysteriously in the masculine bosom. This impulse is the subject of II, 4, the story of Landolfo Rufolo.

Landolfo, who lives in a small coastal town near Salerno, is 'a very rich man indeed. But being dissatisfied with his fortune, he sought to double it' ('disiderando di radoppiarla', 5; p. 136). The suddenness of this impulse or desire (note the verb *disiderare*) is as mysterious as the impulse to love, or possess, that suddenly grips male protagonists in other *novelle*. This impulse is not glossed or dwelt upon. Is this urge to 'acquisition and possession' divinely inspired? It would seem not: for in Aristotle and Dante trade is justified as a cooperative enterprise in which a surplus of goods in one city or region meets a specific lack in another. Landolfo, however, is driven by an individualistic impulse to convert his liquid assets into a 'very large ship' full of cargo and set off on the high seas. When he arrives at Cyprus he discovers no lack to meet his surplus but his own mirror image: a number of ships 'carrying precisely the same kind of goods as those he had brought over himself' (7; p. 137).

Landolfo next exchanges his large merchant ship for a smaller, quicker one and becomes a privateer, dedicated 'to the systematic looting of other people's property, especially that of the Turks' (9; p. 137). This is the purest expression of the impulse that first moved him; its destructive, self-seeking character gains some legitimacy in being turned against the infidel. Once he has robbed and looted enough, Landolfo persuades himself ('a se medesimo dimostrò', 11) to be content and return home. Not bothering to invest his money or acquire a merchant ship, he sails home at breakneck speed. But he is captured and robbed by sailors from Genoa; the Genoese vessel is then itself shipwrecked, and Landolfo is thrown into the sea. He clings to a spar and then to a chest that ('as luck would have it', p. 139) crashes into it. The image of Landolfo clinging to this chest, barely distinguishable from the water that surrounds him (he is almost a sponge, 'quasi una spugna', 22), totally unable to direct his own movements, forms a powerful gloss on the impulse that first sent him to sea. At this point the narrator is unwilling to declare what power, natural or divine, is directing Landolfo's movements: he lands on Corfu, 'either through the will of God or the power of the wind' (22; p. 139).

Landolfo is fished from the sea by an old lady who nurses him back to life; he returns home with the assistance of some cloth-merchants from his native town. On discovering that his chest contains precious jewels, he interprets his experience by reviving the familiar distinction: Fortune has dealt him cruel blows, but God has come to his rescue (27; p. 140). On returning home he discovers that he has, indeed, doubled his fortune. He repays his debts of kindness with punctilious care and 'was no longer interested in commerce' ('mercatare', 30; p. 141).

The impulse to trade in II, 4 inspires a brief, manic interval of adventure on the high seas that interrupts the quiet routine of an ordinary life and vanishes as mysteriously as it had arrived. The recklessness to which it drives Landolfo apparently has little to do with the business of great companies such as the Bardi, who would never dispatch goods without securing a market for them or set sail in the wrong-sized ship. And yet the impulse which moves Landolfo does have an undeniable mythic force: for without it, the great mercantile companies would never have come into existence. Life was simpler and more innocent in the *aetas prima*, the first age of human history when (in Chaucer's words) 'No ship yit karf the wawes grene and blewe; No marchaunt yit ne fette out-landissh ware' (*The Former Age*, 21–2). And yet human history, experienced by the medieval world as a long chronicle of triumphs and disasters, could hardly have begun without such carving of the waves. Even Dante, at the very end of his *Paradiso*, takes his historical bearings from the enterprise or 'impresa' of Jason and his Argonauts, a journey that makes Neptune stare up in amazement as the sea is darkened by the shadow of a ship ('che fé Nettuno ammirar l'ombra d'Argo', XXXIII, 96).

The grand temporal and spatial dimensions of II, 4 are deliberately miniaturized by the *novella* that follows: whereas Lauretta's story covers several years, Fiammetta tells of the events of a single night (II, 5, 2; p. 141). II, 4 tells of a rich man who doubles his money by returning home with precious stones, whereas II, 5 stars a Perugian horse-trader who gains just one stone and recoups his original investment. II, 4 ranges across the whole Mediterranean world, whereas II, 5 is confined to a single city. But the voyage of Andreuccio through the streets, brothels, sewers, markets, churches, and tombs of Naples is just as fantastic as that of Landolfo on the ocean, and takes twice as long to tell.

The city in the *Decameron* is usually represented as an orderly, well-regulated mechanism. The Florentines in II, 1, for example, get themselves into serious trouble by mocking the religious and civic pride of a foreign city, but they survive by employing their knowledge of urban institutions (the watch, the customs house, the court of law). Andreuccio, however, is innocent of all such knowledge: the city controls his movements as if he were a rudderless ship. He (or rather the five hundred gold florins he carries with him) first attracts the attention of a young prostitute, who promises to supply the lack that he experiences in this foreign city ('I was feeling rather lonely here', 26; p. 145). He is charmed by this woman's exotic and sweet-smelling bedchamber (which he

fails to recognize as a workplace). Having been wined and
dined, he steps out to the toilet, treads on a loose board and
falls into the sewer below. As Andreuccio drops into the
'filthy mess', Boccaccio's narrator steps forward with a
learned and elegant gloss: 'Now in order to give you a clearer
picture of what has preceded and what follows, I shall
describe the sort of place it was' (39; p. 147). The ensuing
description of boards rigged between adjacent houses adds
nothing to the narrative action but invites us to dwell on symbolic function: this precarious aerial toilet is like a giant wheel
of Fortune, which transfers Andreuccio's clothes and horse-
trading capital to the woman above and leaves him in the
'bruttura' below.

Boccaccio's narrator, in describing Andreuccio's descent,
sees God at work: 'and God so loved him that no harm was
done in the fall' (38, my translation). This somewhat surprising perception of divine solicitude is strengthened later in the
story: if Andreuccio had not taken that fall he would certainly
have been murdered (60; p. 151). Fortune, we are reminded
again, is a hermeneutic category: it is the interpretation of
events, rather than events themselves, that make an experience good or bad.

As Andreuccio climbs from the sewer we see another aspect
of Fortune: she is the inspiration or Muse of narrative fiction.
For as Andreuccio's seemingly random progress through
night-time Naples becomes ever more surreal and fantastic, so
Boccaccio's control of narrative detail becomes more God-
like and absolute. When the sewage-laden Andreuccio arrives
at a well, for example, we find that 'the bucket has been
removed' (66; p. 151); Andreuccio must shin down the rope
to wash himself clean. The vanished bucket allows Boccaccio
to get Andreuccio to the bottom of the well; he can then
reemerge, apparition-like, to scare off the officers of the
watch. The narrative moves its protagonist forward through
such ingenious contrivances and climaxes with the most
outrageous positioning of all: Andreuccio, wearing a ruby
ring on his finger, is shut in a tomb with a recently deceased
Archbishop. The priest who steps forward to rob this tomb

supplies Andreuccio with the perfect cue for his next narrative act: 'Dead men don't eat the living. I will go in myself' (82; p. 154). Andreuccio, assuming the place of a dead man, reaches up and grabs his legs; the priest screams and runs off as if pursued by one hundred thousand devils.

By the end of II, 5 Fortune has fulfilled the task ascribed to her by Virgil in *Inferno* VII by shifting prosperity and power from group to group in quite dramatic fashion. The prostitute gains Andreuccio's clothes and his five hundred gold florins; Andreuccio gains a ring 'worth more than five hundred gold florins' (63; p. 151). The only loser is the Church, although the Church's capital had been of no social benefit since it was laid in the tomb. This was actually the fate of a great deal of capital in the Middle Ages: merchants were expected to redress the balance of their dubious lifestyles by bequeathing the Church generous amounts of money. But most of this capital was taken out of circulation by being spent on chantries, masses for the dead and ecclesiastical building. The reversal of this movement in II, 5 neatly allegorizes the miraculous vitality of the mercantile economy: capital, unlike the dead Archbishop, has the power to rise from the dead and live again.

Third day: sex, voice and morals

On the first Sunday the storytellers strike camp and move to a beautiful palace, adjoined by a walled garden. This garden (the new site of the storytelling) is full of exotic fragrances, suggestive of the spices of the East, and is of exquisite design: 'If Paradise were constructed on earth' (11; p. 233) this would be it. The Earthly Paradise was an imaginative site that the Middle Ages were content to share with ancient and pagan worlds: here man and woman might enjoy the perfect bliss of natural love. But for the medieval Christian, such a place was also a reminder of loss: since the Fall brought us east of Eden, men and women have never recaptured the idyllic harmony of their former innocent state. All ten tales in the third day are dedicated to the difficult dynamics of masculine – feminine relations. All ten feature attempts (nine successful) at illicit, deceptive or coercive love. Some of these stories, especially the first and last (Masetto among the nuns; Alibech among the hermits) have been found immoral: but every *novella* raises difficult questions about sexual relations and the mores devised to govern them.

Many of the themes developed during the third day were first broached by the final story of day two. In this *novella* an elderly judge marries a pretty young woman but then minimizes physical contact by following an elaborate timetable of religious abstinence: no sex on Sundays or saints' days, in Lent or during certain phases of the moon, etc. The wife, Bartolomea, is abducted by a pirate, Paganino da Mare. The old judge eventually tracks them down, but the wife refuses to recognize him on the grounds that 'you showed very little sign of knowing *me*, when I was living with you' (31; p. 225). This *me* is then realized through a great rush of language, an unstoppable, reasoned torrent of affirmation and abuse. Sexuality, she tells him, demands labour, not abstinence: 'if you had given as many holidays to the workers on your estates as you gave to the one whose job it was to tend my little field, you would never have harvested a single ear of corn' (32; p. 225). She and Paganino, ignoring the religious calendar, 'worked their fingers to the bone' (43; p. 227). The old judge, on hearing this, 'suffered the agonies of the damned' (35; p. 226). He returns home alone and goes mad, repeating a phrase that suggests both frantic activity in the law court and the essential negativity of his outlook: 'There's never any rest for the bar' (42; p. 227).

The judge's madness accompanies the collapse of the structure of denial that orders his life. He realizes his own identity through denying recognition ('conoscimento', 31) to feminine sexuality: but once the wife has gone he has nothing to deny and no identity to speak of. Such emptiness lies at the heart of misogyny: if women did not exist, the misogynist would have nothing to say.

The medieval misogynist had his own rationale for masculine silence: men cannot speak because women never stop talking. Or, more specifically, that women keep quiet until the sexual act loosens their tongue: in II, 10, for example, Bartolomea does not speak until she knows Paganino. (This association between the power and endurance of the female voice and the power and endurance of female sexuality is most famously exemplified by Chaucer's Wife of Bath.) Antifeminist commonplaces are to be found throughout the third day, but so too is a recognition that they are devised to save and protect men from moments of truth and inadequacy in their encounters with women.

In the first *novella* of the third day Masetto, the male protagonist, sets out full of confidence to take care of a whole gardenful of women: 'Once you put me inside that garden of yours' (he says to himself) 'I'll work it better than it's ever been worked before' (18; p. 237). This garden, which belongs to a convent, excites the masculine imagination as a figure of virginal female sexuality ripe for cultivation. Masetto decides that he will be the gardener, the new Adam in this earthly paradise: he takes no warning from the shrunken figure of Nuto, the old Adam who tells of the inexhaustible energy and devilment of the young nuns, who would sometimes 'snatch the very hoe from my hands' (9; p. 235).

Masetto becomes convent gardener by pretending to be a deaf-mute: without speech or hearing he is assumed to be harmless and simple-minded. When female protagonists (such as Alatiel in I, 7) cannot communicate through language they are seen as weak and vulnerable. But Masetto grows more powerful by taking on deafness and silence. Even when he is thought to be sleeping he is in fact awake, enjoying privileged access to secret female conversations. What he hears from the two young nuns who plan to use him sexually confirms long-established masculine wisdom: that what women fear from sex is not loss of virginity or pregnancy but their inability to stop themselves from talking about it afterwards (25–8; p. 238). When the nuns wake him he springs to his feet at once ('incontanente', 31). As he goes off to the woodshed with them he wears a big, imbecilic grin: he is in complete control of the situation.

But as the other nuns become partners ('compagne', 33) in this enterprise, Masetto becomes not the farmer but the farmed. All the women are keen to become shareholders in his smallholding ('partefici . . . del poder di Masetto', 33), but once the Abbess joins in he is worked to exhaustion. And so he breaks his silence to recognize his limits: 'I can't endure it any longer'; 'I'm no longer capable of delivering the goods' (37; p. 240). A new arrangement is made: Masetto is retired from gardening to become the convent's steward; his sexual services are shared out more sparingly. Having fathered 'quite a number of nunlets and monklets', he follows the example of Nuto, the old Adam, by retiring to his native village on a pension.

The male voice speaks, then, only to disclose that masculine sexuality cannot sustain the pretensions of masculine fantasy. In the encounter with female desire it ends with a double *non posso*: 'io non potrei durare'; 'io non posso fare' (37: 'I could not last'; 'I cannot do'). Masetto, like the old judge in the preceding *novella*, must regulate his sex-life by the calendar.

The third day's last *novella* forms a companion piece to the first: we begin with one secular male among female religious and end with a teenage girl among hermits. But Alibech, unlike Masetto, begins as an outsider, a marginal figure: she is an Arab among Christians, a young woman, one of many children. She is led from her home town of Gafsa to the hermits by a child-like appetite for knowledge ('fanciullesco appetito', 6): what, she asks, is the best and easiest way to serve God? One hermit, Rustico, soon recruits her into the familiar structure of sexual denial: he will live with her but resist sexual attraction by way of proving his own 'will of iron' (9; p. 315). This project soon collapses and Rustico makes Alibech his own religio-sexual disciple; they undress and contemplate the mystery of 'the resurrection of the Flesh' (13; p. 316). It is at this point, at the borderline of innocent curiosity and sexual knowledge, that Alibech speaks for the first time: 'Rustico, what is that thing I see sticking out in front of you, which I do not possess?' A brief catechism follows (in which Alibech and Rustico become 'figliuola mia' and 'padre mio') and Alibech learns how the devil is put back into Hell.

Alibech's speaking signals the awakening of a sexual appetite that can never again fall silent or inactive: 'my Hell simply refuses to leave me alone' (29; p. 318). She is hungry for work, but one hermit living on a diet of herbs and water cannot keep her busy: the little he can manage 'was rather like chucking a bean into the mouth of a lion' (30; p. 318).

Both III, 1 and III, 10 represent brilliant responses to the topic proposed for the third day, namely 'people who by dint of their own efforts have achieved an object they greatly desired, or recovered a thing previously lost' (p. 231; rubric). These two *novelle* are particularly concerned with the theme of recovery: Masetto recovers his voice, and Alibech restores the devil to Hell and in so doing recovers the ideal unity of man and woman prescribed by God in Eden − 'they shall be two in one Flesh' (Genesis 2, 24). Both *novelle* develop Edenic themes: Masetto returns to the garden to experience the 'paradise of pleasure' of Genesis 2, 8; Alibech finds that the God-given union of man and woman is 'così dolce cosa' (25). But both protagonists discover post-lapsarian limits. Masetto's speaking, unlike the Adamic naming of Genesis 2, 19–20, reveals weakness: Alibech finds that the ideal gender balance ordained in the paradise garden can no longer be maintained, because of 'a surplus of desire on the one hand and a shortage of power on the other' (31; p. 318).

The Masetto and Alibech stories are both told by masculine storytellers (Filostrato and Dioneo respectively). Both tellers are conscious that the Edenic and myth-making themes developed by their narratives acquire a certain polemical force in being told to a mixed group gathered in a *hortus inclusus*. By the end of the third day, the *brigata* has plainly become divided along lines of gender as Neifile, the third day queen, crowns Filostrato king for the fourth day: 'Now we shall discover whether the wolf can fare any better at leading the sheep than the sheep have fared in leading the wolves' (conclusion, 1; p. 319). Men and women, it seems, are now to be considered as separate species. In the quick-fire gender war that follows, both outgoing queen and incoming king draw their arguments from III, 1 and III, 10. Filostrato says that if men were really wolves and women sheep all women would be Alibechs by now. Neifile replies that if women were Alibechs, men would soon become talking Masettos to save themselves 'when your bones were rattling from exhaustion' (2–3; pp. 319–20). This conflict between genders over powers of sex and voice possessed great comic and mythic potency in the Middle Ages: the same issues are argued out between king and queen in the walled garden of Chaucer's *Merchant's Tale*.

In post-medieval times the Masetto and Alibech stories have been found to be blasphemous or obscene. It is true that when Masetto becomes husband to a convent of nuns he is usurping the place of Christ: but this truth is cheerfully acknowledged by the *novelliere* himself (43; p. 241). This kind of comic substitution is not unusual. In III, 4, for example, a monk persuades a gullible husband to stand staring at the sky with his arms draped over wall-pegs. While this 'fool for love' is imitating Christ on the cross, the monk is in bed with his wife, travelling to 'Paradise' (31; p. 262). Such antics were not, before the Counter-Reformation, thought to pose a threat to the truths of the Christian religion. The Alibech story unnerved English translators for hundreds of years; on approaching 'the resurrection of the flesh' they resorted to Italian, or even French, and the *novella* did not appear in English entire and *intacta* until 1930. And yet if there is anything of dubious moral standing to be found in this *novella* it surely lies at the point where the 1903 Rigg translation thinks it safe to return to English: the fire at Gafsa.

Nobody thinks of searching for Alibech until a fire breaks out in Gafsa, in which 'Alibech's father was burnt to death in his own house along with all his children and every member of his household, so that Alibech inherited the whole of his property' (31; p. 318). The man who finds her and returns her (against her will) to Gafsa is a wastrel called Neerbale who has spent his own fortune and is keen to inherit half of hers. The fire in Gafsa, then, is a crude narrative device to get Alibech back to civilization; the 'volgar motto' (35) of the devil in Hell can then enter circulation, cross the ocean to Italy and hence provide the raw material for Dioneo's *novella*. Storytellers often take drastic steps to enforce narrative closure. It is not unusual to kill off minor characters to free up legacies, marriage partners, jobs, etc.: at the end of III, 1 Filostrato kills off the nuns' steward so that Masetto can take his place. But it does seem excessive to incinerate an entire family in a single sentence.

We should note, however, that this excess exemplifies Dioneo's privileged talent for subversion, for flaunting the decorums of storytelling. And such abuse of literary conventions, if such it is, pales in comparison with that practised by the masculine protagonist of III, 6. In this *novella* a nobleman, Ricciardo Minutolo, employs stratagems familiar from Dante's *Vita nuova* to seduce a woman who has no interest in him. Like the love-struck Dante among the women with 'intelligence of love', Ricciardo learns the truth of his situation from a female source: a kinswoman tells him that his love for Catella is hopeless because she is jealously devoted to her husband. Ricciardo uses this intelligence first to allay suspicions (he follows the Dantean tactic of adopting a screen lady) and then to play on Catella's weakness by convincing her that her husband has a rendezvous with Ricciardo's wife in a bath-house. Catella substitutes herself for Ricciardo's wife, but it is of course Ricciardo who meets her in the darkened room. Catella makes a long, impassioned speech of denunciation to (she thinks) her husband. This speech is worth nothing, but Ricciardo keeps silent and takes secret, inward pleasure in letting it run on ('in se medesimo godeva di queste parole', 39; p. 275). Before revealing his real identity he grips her tightly so that she cannot escape; after revealing it he puts his hand over her mouth so she cannot scream. All this is justified by the hoariest of literary commonplaces: 'Love has taught me' (42; p. 276).

The next *novella* sees another love-struck nobleman, Tedaldo, developing and controlling a similarly complex pattern of deception. It ends with Tedaldo stage-managing a civic spectacle designed to reconcile all parties. Throwing off his pilgrim's disguise to reveal himself resplendent in green taffeta, Tedaldo tears dresses of mourning from wives and sisters, reconciles family with family, husband with wife. And yet this is a flawed public ceremony, since Tedaldo never intends to renounce his own private deception, his affair with the woman whose husband he saved from the gallows.

Ricciardo and Tedaldo succeed in achieving their desired objects entirely (to quote from the third day rubric) 'by dint of their own efforts'. They succeed not so much by battling with Fortune as by refusing to believe in her: Tedaldo believes that it was some human agency that set his lady against him and after seven years he discovers who this person was. Their mastery of Fortune, their control of historical contingency, is then demonstrated by their absolute mastery of women. These tales of wilful noblemen bring us closer to absolutist myths of power and a Machiavellian vision of Fortune. The imaginative world they evoke, in which the female voice counts for nothing, adumbrate forms of moral and political corruption never dreamed of in the innocent, Edenic narratives of Masetto and Alibech.

Fourth day (introduction): Boccaccio's apology for Florentine prose

Boccaccio begins the fourth day by suddenly reappearing *in propria persona* as author to share his current difficulties with his primary audience, his 'carissime donne'. Medieval authors, unlike realist novelists, were generally keen to share the technical and ethical difficulties that attend their writing: Chaucer makes a similar intervention in opening book II of *Troilus and Criseyde*; Dante addresses his readers periodically throughout his *Commedia*. Boccaccio begins by confiding that his *novelle* (those already in circulation) have stirred up a fierce wind, a storm of envious resentment. His authorship has been found objectionable on five counts: that he is excessively fond of women; that he is too old to write of and for women; that he should spend his time with the Muses on Parnassus (writing serious works rather than frivolous ones); that there is no money to be made in *novelle*; that these *novelle* are not consistent with the facts (introduction 5–7; pp. 325–6).

By assembling this odd assortment of objections Boccaccio finds occasion to evaluate the status and orientation of his *Decameron*. His most famous defence of literary values, which dates from the same post-plague period, is his *Genealogy of the Gentile Gods*, books XIV–XV. But the Latin *Genealogia* celebrates the inspired, transcendent power of Latin poetry: the *Decameron* is in Florentine prose. Despite Dante's championing of the vernacular in both theory and practice (*De vulgari eloquentia* and the *Commedia*, respectively) medieval critics still tended to doubt that literary works with serious pretensions could be written in Italian. This assumption actually hardened in the course of the fourteenth century (with the rise of the humanist movement): Dante's son Pietro, like most Trecento commentators, chose Latin for his commentary on the *Commedia*. Prose (from the Latin *prorsus*, straightforward) was seen as less sophisticated and less inspired than poetry. By writing in Italian prose, then, Boccaccio is doing women's work: inspired by women, he writes about women in a language that women will understand. Such was the rationale for authorship of the *Decameron* that we saw Boccaccio adumbrating in his *Proemio*.

Now, rather than attempting to develop theoretical arguments on the powers of the vernacular (as he does elsewhere in his writings on Dante), Boccaccio simply defers all objections and turns to storytelling: the medium itself (the suggestion is) will answer its critics. This manoeuvre is achieved with a simply turned phrase that is itself (with the modulation between pronouns and the subsequent isolation of the infinitive verb) eloquent testimony to the untranslatable beauty and clarity of the vernacular: 'mi piace in favor di me raccontare' (11; 'I should like to strengthen my case by recounting . . . a story', p. 326).

The story (or part-story) that follows explores the interrelationship of love and language as forces of nature. Filippo

Balducci, a Florentine, loves his wife for as long as she lives. When she dies ('it happens to us all eventually', 13; p. 326) Filippo responds to this natural tragedy by withdrawing from the world to a hermitage on Mount Asinaio with his infant son. (There actually was a monastery on Mount Asinaio, to the north of Florence, founded by middle-class Florentine men wishing to flee from the world. We should note that the name Asinaio is derived from 'asino', meaning 'ass' and hence 'fool'.) Filippo raises his son in the isolation of a cave, taking 'very great care not to let him see any worldly things' and 'forever telling him about the glory of the life eternal' (15; p. 327). When the boy is eighteen, Filippo finally allows him to accompany him to Florence, confident that years of religious instruction will save him from worldly temptations: that nurture will prove stronger than nature.

The boy is amazed by the city and demands that his father name each new sight. This naming process recalls Genesis 2, 19, where Adam puts a name to each creature of the new Creation. Naming (for the Middle Ages) entailed more than matching a thing with an arbitrary linguistic sign: the name of a thing participates in its meaning. So it is that the boy's appetite for knowledge and understanding is satisfied by the father's naming: 'Once his father had answered one of his questions, his curiosity was satisfied and he went on to ask about something else' (20; p. 327). But when the son sees a *brigata* of beautiful young women, the father twice betrays this process: he first gives a false name ('They are called goslings') and then tries to put an end to language altogether ('hold your tongue'). He ends with an obscure metaphor (about where goslings keep their bills and what they feed on) that represents a withdrawal from public communication: the son does not possess the knowledge that can uncover the obscene meaning of the father's words. As he speaks these last words the father recognizes his own defeat: 'he realized that his wits [ingegno] were no match for Nature' (29; p. 328).

Boccaccio's part-*novella* may be read as a mirror image of the Alibech story which immediately precedes it: having seen

a young girl leaving the city to discover sexuality among hermits, we now encounter a young boy leaving his hermitage to
discover sexuality in the city. The awakening of sexual energy
is thereby realized as a universal phenomenon that strains
(and exceeds) the resources of language and narrative:
perhaps this is why Balducci's son, who so strongly desires to
match things with names, is not himself named (so remaining
a universalized masculine subject). It is also through the process of naming, we may recall, that Adam discovers the
singularity of masculine identity as the lack of women: 'The
man gave names to all cattle, to the birds of the air, and to
every wild animal; but for the man himself no suitable partner
was found' (Genesis 2, 20).

When Dante meets Adam in *Paradiso* XXVI, he learns that
the language spoken in Eden was a vernacular, a language
that changes with time: 'And that is fitting', Adam says, 'for
the usage of mortals is like a leaf on a branch, which goes
away and another comes' (137–8). Latin, the medievals
thought, was immune to the erosions of time: this made it the
appropriate medium for the expression of transcendent
truths. But human experience, as Dante's Adam suggests, is
lived out through time: the vernacular, therefore, is uniquely
appropriate for the expression of human experience because
it shares the organic character of human lives, the narrative
sequence of birth, growth and death. When Balducci refuses
to countenance the natural phenomenon of his wife's death,
he commits himself to a lonely path that leads away from
human society and ends with the refusal of language itself.
And, by a reverse logic, when Boccaccio commits himself to
a language that a whole society can understand, he is signalling his willingness to face up to death and disaster, to accept
the transitory and imperfect terms in which human history is
made. This was a vital commitment for the survivors of 1348.

But does this commitment to writing prose in the Florentine
vernacular in the most humble and unassuming style ('in
fiorentin volgare e in prosa . . . in istilo umilissimo e rimesso',
3; p. 325) suggest that Boccaccio has renounced the possibility
of his work transcending or outlasting the historical moment

of its composition? Once he has completed his part-*novella*, Boccaccio turns to face his critics in playful mood: he responds to their five objections, but in such a way as to differentiate his writing from their expectations of it. He insists on the naturalness of his writing for women and of the love for women that causes him to write. But there are hints, too, that his Florentine prose may be inspired, at times, by a certain transcendent power: the Muses may have been looking over his shoulder; poets find spiritual sustenance in their songs (36–8; p. 330). By associating himself with poets in the *Decameron*, Boccaccio concedes that his language is not entirely natural after all: it is, as we have noted, a native tongue that has extended its capacities by learning from Latin prose, particularly the *cursus*. Such a synthesis approaches Dante's ideal of an illustrious vernacular (*volgare illustre*), a language that has infused the learnedness and sophistication of Latin but retains the immediate expressive vitality of a vernacular. It may even share some of the imaginative and social potency that Boccaccio ascribes to *poetria* in his *Genealogia*, where he declares that 'this fervour of poesy . . . can arm kings, marshal them for war, launch whole fleets from their docks, nay, counterfeit sky, land, sea, adorn young maidens with flowery garlands . . .' (and so on: XIV, 7). But he stops short of suggesting that the language of the *Decameron* can compete or be equated with Latin poetry. Instead, through a brilliant recuperation of his opening metaphor, he suggests that his writing achieves a momentary but glorious transcendence. Figuring himself as dust, the stuff that Adam is made of, Boccaccio imagines himself borne aloft by the very gale of criticism that his critics blow in his direction:

For whatever happens, my fate can be no worse than that of the fine-grained dust, which, when a gale blows, either stays on the ground or is carried aloft, in which case it is frequently deposited upon the heads of men, upon the crowns of kings and emperors, and even upon high palaces and lofty towers, whence, if it should fall, it cannot sink lower than the place from which it was raised.
(40; p. 331)

Fourth day: Love and feudal aristocracy

The choice of theme for the fourth day falls to Filostrato, who nominates 'the one which applies most closely to myself, namely *those whose love ended unhappily*' (III conclusion, 6; p. 320). This call to confront and anatomize human misery puts a severe strain on the storytellers since their storytelling was devised to distract attention from the misery of the Black Death. Throughout the fourth day the *brigata* remains faithful to its ground-rule of following the wishes of its monarch-for-the-day. But it also struggles to find ways of humouring these wishes without allowing them to exhaust the emotional resources of the *brigata*: the group must not be infected or pulled down by Filostrato's personal unhappiness.

In thinking of unhappy love, the minds of Boccaccio's Florentine storytellers run to a certain form of social organization in specific regions: feudal aristocracy in Provence and the south. Love in these circumstances assumes the form of an absolute, abstract power that drives men and women to violent and uncompromising extremes. Boccaccio's *novelle* make it quite clear that such love, in its social effects, is immensely wasteful and destructive. But, ironically enough, these tales of disastrous love have been among the most popular and widely imitated of Boccaccio's *novelle*: one thinks of Dryden (IV, 1; the Ghismonda story), Keats (IV, 5; the pot of basil) and of Pound, whose version of the Cabestanh story (IV, 9; *Cantos* IV) brilliantly recaptures the claustrophobic, uncompromising world of Boccaccio's fourth day. The father in Pound's *Cantos* tells his daughter that she has eaten the heart of her lover, Cabestanh. The daughter, absolutely unflinching, refuses to flatter him with a show of emotion and simply mirrors back his words (only intonation can make a difference) before defenestrating herself:

> 'It is Cabestan's heart in the dish.'
> 'It is Cabestan's heart in the dish?
> No other taste shall change this.' (IV, 21–3)

It is not likely that Pound is borrowing directly from

Boccaccio here, although Boccaccio's *construction* of feudal erotics became so widely disseminated that some influence, direct or indirect, was inevitable. The most influential and most harrowing of all these *novelle* comes first: the story of Tancredi, Guiscardo and Ghismonda. This is set in Norman times at Salerno, an ancient city to the south-east of Naples that fell to Robert Guiscard in 1076. There was a Norman prince called Tancredi, but he never ruled at Salerno. Boccaccio's fourth day *novelle* strive not for historical precision, but rather for a more general evocation of a bygone (but not too distant) feudal epoch. They draw from Boccaccio's experience of court society at Angevin Naples (which had absorbed the cultural legacy of the earlier Norman occupation); they reflect his observation of aristocratic mores not only at Naples but also in Florence, where a feudal-derived nobility continued to exert an active (and often destructive) role within the Florentine body politic.

The first *novella* (narrated by Fiammetta) is doom-laden from the start. The rubric summarizing its action foretells the death of both young protagonists and the opening period pictures Tancredi's blood-covered hands and declares that it would have been better for him had Ghismonda, his only child, never been born (3; p. 332). By the time Ghismonda has selected Guiscardo as her lover (3–6, less than a page of narrative), all the elements for future disaster have been locked into place with no signs of the behavioural flexibility that might avert it.

Tancredi, it is said, 'was as passionately fond of his daughter as any father who ever lived'. The hints of incestuous motivation that run through this *novella* (and many others like it) issue from the collapsing of the political into the personal that obtains in despotic regimes: Tancredi cannot bear to see another man share his daughter's affections because she is his only heir; a man who shared his daughter would threaten to share the power of the princedom that Tancredi, at present, uniquely embodies. Ghismonda, we should note, is initially considered entirely within the ambit of her father's power and identity: she is not actually named until quite late in the *novella*. It seems odd, then, that Tancredi should have agreed, albeit unwillingly, to Ghismonda's marrying the Duke of Capua. This detail, I would suggest, is dictated by narrative (rather than psychological) logic: if Ghismonda had never left her father's side, her sexual appetite would never have been awakened and she would not now need a lover. Such, at least, was the theory of female desire that Ghismonda quotes back to her father later on: 'I am full of amorous longings', she says, 'intensified beyond belief by my marriage' (34; p. 337).

The intensity of Ghismonda's passions never exceeds her extraordinary powers of rational control. She studies the behaviour of several candidate lovers before settling on one, Guiscardo, 'a man of exceedingly humble birth [di nazione assai umile] but noble in character and bearing' (6; p. 333). Once she has chosen Guiscardo her passions are fiercely inflamed ('fieramente s'accese': the term 'fiera' − fierce, wild, cruel − is the opening word of the *novella*, where it describes the subject matter of the fourth day as 'fiera materia'). Guiscardo is soon won over and the lovers put their minds to engineering a liaison. The public space of court society which had allowed them to make eye contact now frustrates their desire for private communication. Soon, however, their desires are recognized by Love, an allegorical personification engendered by the pressured emotional atmosphere of courtly society. There is, it appears, a secret stairway to the lady's bedroom that is all but forgotten: 'but Love [Amore], to whose eyes nothing remains concealed, had reminded the enamoured lady of its existence' (9; p. 333). This stairway leads down to a grotto that is hollowed out under the hill on which the palace stands; it is entered from a shaft in the hillside that is covered over with brambles. Guiscardo waits for nightfall, dons a suit of leather, lowers himself through the brambles, waits in the grotto and then ascends the secret staircase to join the lady in her bedroom. The boudoir, with its two entrances, now becomes a contested, intermediate realm: one door leads to the public domain of court society, and the other opens out to the wild side, a subterranean world of illicit desire.

The happiness granted to Ghismonda and Guiscardo by one personification, Love, soon attracts the envy of another, 'Fortune, who brought about a calamity, turning the joy of the two lovers into tears and sorrow' (15; p. 334). Ghismonda exploits the patterned regularity of courtly life by leaving her ladies-in-waiting outside her door and meeting Guiscardo in her bedroom. But Tancredi, as ruler, is free to dispense with such patterns and enter the bedchamber whenever he sees fit. On finding Ghismonda absent from her room one day he decides to wait for her and rests his head on her bedside; he draws the bedclothes around himself 'as though to conceal himself there on purpose' (17; p. 335) and falls asleep. When he awakes he discovers Guiscardo and his daughter making love: the sequence of his waking and hearing and seeing is marked with punctilious care by three consecutive verbs ('Tancredi si svegliò e sentì e vide', 18). He controls his impulse to cry out and plays the voyeur for a long time ('per lungo spazio', 20).

When Guiscardo has left by the door to the grotto and Ghismonda by the door to the court, Tancredi finds a third way out of the bedchamber (thereby signalling the irregularity of his presence there) by climbing out of the window. Guiscardo is arrested as he emerges from the hole in the ground, struggling through the brambles in his leather suit like some desperate insect. He is taken in secret to Tancredi, who upbraids him for the outrageous and shameful act he saw him committing 'against that which belonged to me' (p. 335). With this awkward, circumlocutious construction ('la quale nelle mie cose fatta m'hai', 22) Tancredi represents Guiscardo as the outsider who has violated both Ghismonda and himself, fused together as 'le mie cose'. Guiscardo counters this verbal strategy by isolating both himself and Tancredi as equal subjects (sharing a plural verb) of a greater *signore*: 'Neither you nor I can resist the power of Love' (p. 335; 'Amor può troppo più che né voi né io possiamo', 23). This is the last we hear from Guiscardo, but his strategy of isolating Ghismonda from Tancredi is adopted by Ghismonda herself for the remainder of the *novella*.

The *novella*'s centrepiece is an extended interchange between father and daughter. Tancredi tries to wring some empathetic or at least emotional response from Ghismonda by speaking of how he is tormented by the memory of her 'yielding to' (p. 336: the image is cruder and more graphic, 'sottoporti' (26), literally 'putting yourself under') a man of extremely low social degree ('di vilissima condizione', 27). Tancredi positions himself as the honest arbiter, pulled between paternal affection and personal outrage; he ends by weeping like a child 'who had been soundly beaten' (29; p. 336). Ghismonda denies herself the weakness ('viltà') of an emotional response, counters all power he might have over her with a double negative and rejects his authority as father by employing his proper name ' "Tancredi", she said, "I am resolved neither to contradict you nor to implore your forgiveness" ' (p. 337; 'Tancredi, né a negare né a pregare son disposta', 31). In what follows, Ghismonda is concerned not to explain herself to her father, but rather (like many medieval heroines) to explain herself to us, her readers in posterity ('defender la fama mia', 31). She begins by affirming her love for Guiscardo, employing five forms of the verb *amare* (past, present and future) in one short sentence (32; p. 337). She speaks dispassionately of how sexual desire ('concupiscibile disidero', 34) is intensified in women by marriage, and of how Love and Fortune conspire to fulfil such desire. She develops an ethical theory that disassociates nobility from accidents of birth and ties it to standards of behaviour (a theory eagerly adopted by the Florentine middle classes). And finally, exercising 'a will of iron', she sends Tancredi away: 'Now get you hence to shed your tears among the women' (45; p. 339).

The overriding irony here is that Ghismonda's rejection of Tancredi reveals her to be her father's daughter: each is as fiercely uncompromising as the other in their attachment to the rigidly defined mores of a feudal aristocracy. Guiscardo, at this stage, is still alive: but there is no question of Ghismonda even inquiring after him, let alone begging for his life.

Tancredi responds to Ghismonda's disquisition by sending

her the heart of Guiscardo in a golden chalice. Ghismonda thanks her father for the gift and weeps silent tears over the heart, 'suppressing all sound of womanly grief' (55; p. 340). These tears, which gush forth like water from a fountain, are tears of will rather than emotion. She adds a poisonous potion to the chalice, drinks it, lies on the bed with Guiscardo's heart on her heart and is waiting to die when Tancredi arrives. Ghismonda recognizes that Tancredi's cruel strategy was to make her see Guiscardo naked, out of his body, 'with the eyes of my body' (51; p. 340). Now she forces her father to see again that which he cannot bear to remember, namely the sight of Ghismonda beneath Guiscardo on the bed. Tancredi bursts into tears, but Ghismonda rejects his weeping by suddenly making her father, rather than herself, the spectacle to be marvelled at: 'Who ever saw [chi vide mai] anyone but you weep on achieving his wishes?' (60). Ghismonda then dies, leaving 'this life of sorrow behind her' (61; p. 342).

The closest approximations in English to the sombre, claustrophobic mood of this *novella* are to be found in Chaucer: in the fierce and uncompromising adherence to ancient and absolute codes of behaviour in *The Knight's Tale* (which is based on Boccaccio's *Teseida*) and in *The Physician's Tale*, where paternal jealousy and an archaic, narrowly defined aristocratic code of honour conspire to kill a young girl. The thought of Virginius killing Virginia, father killing daughter, is more than Chaucer's Host can bear: he needs a stiff drink and an entertaining story to save himself from cardiac arrest (VI, 312–17; he is saved by the obliging Pardoner). The effect of the Ghismonda story upon Boccaccio's *brigata* is similarly devastating. Filostrato, however, derives a grim satisfaction from it and asks Pampinea to follow with another of these cruel tales ('fieri ragionamenti' p. 342; IV, 2, 3). Pampinea, the oldest of the women and the originator of the *brigata* structure, recognizes that her companions need 'to laugh and be merry' if they are to recover from the death of Ghismonda. And so, being more loyal to the general welfare of the *brigata* than to Filostrato's idiosyncrasies, she tells the story of Frate Alberto and the feather-brained merchant's wife, Monna Lisetta. Lisetta's chief cause for anxiety is that her lover, the Archangel Gabriel (Frate Alberto in disguise), may be too great an admirer of the Blessed Virgin Mary: she has seen Gabriel kneeling before Mary in lots of paintings (25; p. 347).

Pampinea's narrative is a brilliant *tour de force* of comic storytelling: this is the *novella* that Erich Auerbach selects to exemplify Boccaccian narrative in his *Mimesis*. Part of the pleasure of this *novella* comes from our sense of release in moving north from the confined spaces of a feudal castle to the open spaces of the city-state of Venice; from Ghismonda's tightly reasoned *ragionamenti* to Lisetta's Venetian dialect. Boccaccio takes full advantage of this Venetian setting: when Frate Alberto is trapped in a bedroom in his Archangel's disguise by Lisetta's irate relatives he is able to fly out of the window (and swim to safety via a Venetian canal). If this *novella* has a hero it is the city-state, a social structure that is able to identify and uncover the 'thief, pander, swindler and murderer' (10; p. 344) who has penetrated it from the outside: Frate Alberto's deceptions are first publicized by gossip that circulates through the city and reaches the Rialto, the centre for mercantile exchange; they are finally uncovered at the Piazza San Marco, a public space formed by the intersection of the city's most important civic and ecclesiastical buildings. The transition from tragedy in Salerno to comedy in Venice, then, is achieved by moving from the narrow radius of feudal polity to the broader, more inclusive circle of the mercantile city-state.

Filostrato is not amused by Pampinea's story; he instructs Lauretta to tell 'a better tale' (meaning a more serious one). Lauretta's narrative opens at Marseilles, which is described as an ancient and illustrious coastal city in Provence that is now in decline (IV, 3, 8; p. 354). Her protagonists soon sail south and the narrative quickly returns us to the theme of disastrous love. Following three *novelle* of love and death in the south which once again exemplify the most destructive and self-destructive extremes of human behaviour (IV, 3, 4 and 5), we have three *novelle* set in the north (IV, 6, 7 and 8). These northern *novelle* are much less harrowing: the tale set in Brescia (IV, 6) does not end in death, and the two set in Florence strive for effects of pathos rather than high tragedy by featuring lovers from the lower orders: two wool-workers (IV, 7) and an apprentice merchant who falls for a tailor's daughter who marries a tentmaker (IV, 8). We then return to Provence for the Cabestanh story (IV, 9, a very short *novella*) and then come full circle by revisiting Salerno (IV, 10). Dioneo's Salerno features the city rather than the palace and is full of farcical machinations: the dramatic climax comes with a cry of 'Burglars! Burglars!' that sends a whole neighbourhood scurrying through doorways and across rooftops (IV, 10, 28; p. 397). The laughter which follows this *novella* finally disperses the cloud of melancholy first engendered by Tancredi's Salerno.

It is evident, by the end of the fourth day, that the towering and uncompromising passions of aristocratic love can exert a ruinous effect on social and political order. The young lovers who sail from Marseilles to Crete and attempt to ape an aristocratic lifestyle are obviously bound for disaster (IV, 3, 19; p. 357). The young Sicilian prince who falls for a Tunisian princess and recklessly pursues her across the high seas is evidently putting the delicate balance of Christian – Arab relations under severe strain: his own father is compelled to behead him for political rather than personal reasons (IV, 4). Filostrato's appetite for such narratives also poses a threat to the *brigata*'s well-being. Before embarking on the Tancredi story, Fiammetta had speculated that Filostrato must be driven by some deep-seated personal animus in forcing the *brigata* to address this theme of misery in love. At the end of the fourth day, when Filostrato names her as queen, Fiammetta commands Filostrato to sing the obligatory *canzone* so that 'no other day than this may be blighted by your woes' (conclusion 9; p. 402). Filostrato complies, and it becomes apparent that his sickness and resentment stem from his being deserted by one of the *brigata*'s women.

The *brigata*, then, retains its integrity by allowing Filostrato to have his day (and no more than his day) and retains its sanity by moving north at intervals to palliate the tales of disastrous aristocratic love that unfold in the south. Such narratives are best left in the south (not reenacted by Florentines) because the fierce and uncompromising pursuit of love has an unhealthy tendency to breed fierce and uncompromising habits in the conduct of political life.

Fifth day: romance, class difference, social negotiation

The topic for the fifth day, chosen by Fiammetta as an antidote or corrective to Filostrato's unhealthy preoccupations, concerns 'the adventures of lovers who survived calamities or misfortunes and attained a state of happiness' (IV, conclusion 5; p. 402). In most instances, the happiness of these lovers is initially forbidden or frustrated by the hierarchy of class differences which governs their societies. This forces them to leave their homeland and embark upon a series of adventures as exiles on foreign territory. These adventures in foreign realms, the very stuff of romance, represent not so much a threat to their love as a means through which they can negotiate a return to the homeland and be accepted as a permanent alliance, a new household within the established social structure. This persistent interest in reconciling differences in social standing might seem, to some modern readers, positively unromantic: Boccaccio is thinking more like the (illegitimate) son of a merchant and a student of canon law than like the author of courtly romance. But such an interest clearly answers to the experience of the *Decameron*'s first readers in their struggle to situate themselves in the complex class and status systems of Trecento Florence.

One of the fifth day storytellers speaks of herself as roaming through ('spaziandomi') a specific geographical area in her storytelling (5, 3). The fifth day sees a good deal of wandering about, both within specific *novelle* and between one *novella* and the next: four are set in Mediterranean world south of Naples, one in Rome, three in Romagna, one in (just outside) Florence and one in Perugia. Such a range of locations offers us a variety of social formations and hence a variety of narrative paths to the common point of closure, the state of happiness in love. We begin where the fourth day ends, in the south.

The first *novella*, supposedly drawn from 'the chronicles of the ancient Cypriots', sets out to exemplify 'the sacredness, the power, and the beneficial effects of love' (1, 2; p. 406). The class difference which drives this narrative is actually embodied by a single person: Cimone, the son of a 'nobilissimo' nobleman, has the outstandingly attractive and powerful physique that nobles were meant to have but he also has the mind of a moron. The clearest sign of his imbecility is his preference for living with farmworkers in the country-side rather than with citizens in the city; the 'refined senti-ment' (p. 407) that Cimone's teachers try to beat into him is, in the Italian, 'cittadinesco piacere', literally 'citizenly pleasure' (2, 8). The civilizing process begins belatedly for Cimone when he sees a beautiful, near-naked girl asleep in the woods. Leaning on his stick ('bastone', 8), Cimone feels the first stirrings of intellectual life as he gazes at the girl and distinguishes her bodily parts ('distinguer le parti di lei') as a poet might divide up a poem: hair, brow, nose, mouth, neck, arms, bosom (9; p. 407). He gives up the countryside forth-with, returns to his father's house and devotes himself to a course of study (recognizably Italian proto-humanist) that makes him 'the most graceful, refined, and versatile young man on the island of Cyprus' (20; p. 409).

From this point on, the narrative parallels many of the fourth day tales of southern provenance. Cimone's beloved, who bears the ill-starred name of Iphigenia, is shipped off to marry Pasimondas, a nobleman of Rhodes. Cimone sails off in pursuit, boards the Rhodian ship 'like a raging lion' and strikes down the opposition 'like so many sheep' (28; p. 410). He is then captured and imprisoned at Rhodes but escapes in time to break in on the wedding feast of Iphigenia and Pasimondas. The bride is abducted, the groom has his skull crushed by an immense blow from Cimone and the wedding hall is left 'full of blood, tumult, tears, and sadness' (69;

p. 416). Cimone sails back to Cyprus and 'lived happily ever after with his bride in the land of his birth' (71; p. 417). With these final words the *novella* assures us that our hero has taken his rightful place as a noble among the nobles of Cypriot society. But this assurance is compromised somewhat by the sudden reappearance of a key signifier at the *novella*'s dramatic climax, namely the big stick or 'bastone' which Cimone carried about with him during his country days. This 'bastone' is wielded by Pasimondas as he runs to the defence of Iphigenia at the wedding feast (67; p. 416). Cimone's killing of Pasimondas might be read as a final rejection of his own former self. And yet the very savagery of this blow (Pasimondas is half-decapitated) suggests that Cimone will never quite forget the ways of the wild beast ('modi più convenienti a bestia che a uomo', 4) that guided his behaviour at the outset. This *novella* (one of the few set in a far-off past) might be read, then, as an attempt to imagine a mythological predecessor for all those masculine figures in the fourth day who embody both educated refinement and animal savagery in their pursuit of love.

The second *novella* features Gostanza and Martuccio, two lovers from Lipari, an island near Sicily. Their marriage is forbidden by the girl's father because it would bring about a mismatch of social degree: she is from a noble family and he is a craftsman. This leads each of the lovers in turn to abandon their native island: Martuccio leaves in a pirate ship, determined to raise his fortunes by plundering the coast of north Africa; Gostanza, convinced that Martuccio has perished at sea, casts herself adrift in a rudderless boat, determined to die. Martuccio, after a spell of imprisonment, becomes military adviser to the king of Tunis; Gostanza is cast ashore on the Barbary coast and joins a community of women making objects of silk, palm and leather. When the two lovers are finally reunited their class identities have been reversed: Martuccio enjoys noble status and Gostanza is a craftworker. Gostanza now has to prove to the king that she has the right to marry Martuccio. The lovers, having left their homeland in separate vessels, now return to Lipari in the same ship and celebrate their wedding 'with great pomp and splendour' (47; p. 423).

The third *novella* matches the son of a noble Roman family with the daughter of a plebeian. When the noble father intimidates his plebeian counterpart (the daughter must not marry the son) the lovers elope. Eight miles out of Rome, however, they take a wrong turn and get lost in a forest. This forest, which bristles with friendly or unfriendly soldiers, brigands, wolves, peasants, shepherds and aristocrats, functions like the high seas in other *novelle* as a marginal realm that enables a mismatched couple to renegotiate their way back into a hierarchically minded society. This view of romance as social negotiation is developed most powerfully by the three *novelle* set in Romagna, the region to the east of Tuscany in which Boccaccio had worked during the years immediately preceding the plague. The most famous of them is V, 4, the *novella* in which Filostrato tries to make amends for the gloomy monotony he insisted on during the fourth day. The chief prop of his strategy for raising laughs is a single trope that is worked extremely hard in the course of the *novella*: the nightingale that sings in the garden. Filostrato's heroine, Caterina, is the only daughter of an elderly father, destined (her father hopes) to marry 'the son of some great nobleman' (5; p. 432). She promptly falls for Ricciardo, a young man from her own domestic circle who persuades her 'to come to the balcony overlooking your father's garden' (12; p. 432). Caterina eventually persuades her parents to allow her to sleep on this balcony so that the nightingale can 'sing me off to sleep' (21; p. 433).

This balcony above the garden, which is located just outside the father's bedroom, is the most ingenious and most precarious of all the fifth day's marginal sites. Caterina is her father's garden: in her all his future hopes reside. When Ricciardo's nightingale enters and sings in this garden all the old father's hopes seem ruined. But as the old man gazes at the two lovers sleeping naked on his balcony (Caterina holding Ricciardo's member) he does some quick calculations: 'Ricciardo is a rich young man and comes from noble stock. . .

If he wishes to leave this house unscathed he will first have to marry our daughter, so that he will have to put his nightingale into his own cage and into no other' (38; p. 435). Ricciardo agrees to these conditions and lives happily ever after, 'caging nightingales by the score, day and night, to his heart's content' (49; p. 437).

In V, 9 a different bird becomes the object of desire in another narrative that brings the symbols and ideals of courtly love into contact with more pragmatic social principles. This is the only fifth day *novella* set in Florence: or rather, just outside Florence, since its protagonist becomes so poor in courting a noble married lady that he can no longer afford to live in the city. Federigo degli Alberighi, the failed suitor, lives in poverty on a tiny farm with a solitary symbolic reminder of his noble status: a falcon 'of the finest breed in the whole world' (7; p. 464). His lady-love, Monna Giovanna, becomes a widow; her young son inherits all the goods and property of her very rich husband, with the stipulation that if he should die without issue everything will pass to the mother. Mother and son visit their country estate every summer. This adjoins Federigo's farm, and the young boy soon becomes enamoured of Federigo's falcon. When the boy falls ill the mother repeatedly asks him if there is anything he needs; she will 'move heaven and earth' to obtain whatever he might want. Finally the boy replies: 'Mother, if you could arrange for me to have Federigo's falcon I believe I should soon get better' (13; p. 465). Next morning the mother sets out for Federigo's farm.

Monna Giovanna's mission should be successful because it is evident that Federigo would do anything at all for her. But it ends in failure: her son never sees the falcon and he dies soon afterwards. What kills the boy, in short, are the protocols of noble and courtly behaviour. The first chance to save the child is missed when Giovanna adopts the duplicitous rhetoric of *politesse*: instead of telling Federigo that she needs his falcon she says she has come 'to make amends for the harm you have suffered on my account, by loving me more than you ought to have done' (20; p. 466; Federigo, ironically, will soon reenact this fault of excessive love by killing the falcon). The second chance passes when Federigo insists on treating his tiny cottage as if it were a palace: he leads the lady through the house to the garden where she is to wait while he supervises the cooking. The third chance is lost because Federigo, on realizing that he has nothing to cook, is too proud 'to beg assistance from his own farmer' (25; p. 466). He wrings the neck of his falcon and the last symbol of his nobility becomes dead meat. And when the bird dies, so does the child's last hope: when Monna Giovanna unknowingly eats the falcon she is, in effect, eating her son.

Federigo is mortified to learn that he has destroyed that which his lady-love came to ask of him. Giovanna reproaches him for his rashness, but she is soon 'lost in admiration for his magnanimity of spirit, which no amount of poverty had managed to diminish, nor ever would' (37; p. 468). When her son dies her brothers urge her to remarry, 'since not only had she been left a vast fortune but she was still a young woman' (39; p. 469). Giovanna insists that she will marry Federigo or nobody; her brothers, after mocking Federigo's poverty, 'hand her over to him'. The *novella* closes by assuring us that Federigo, 'finding himself married to this great lady with whom he was so deeply in love, and very rich into the bargain . . . managed his affairs more prudently' (43; p. 469).

Before embarking on this *novella* Boccaccio's narrator, Filomena, took considerable pains to emphasize that her narrative is deeply rooted in both the historical and the story-telling traditions of Florence: she heard it from Coppo di Borghesi Domenichi 'who once lived in our city and possibly lives there still' (he does: this well-known Florentine politician survived the plague and lived on until 1353). Her protagonist bears one of the most ancient and famous names in Florentine history: the Alberighi had lived in the Porta San Pietro district near to the church of Santa Maria degli Alberighi and were neighbours of the Alighieri. But even during the time of Dante's great-great-grandfather, Cacciaguida, the Alberighi were already in decline (*Paradiso* XVI, 89); by the early Trecento they were (according to Giovanni Villani) extinct.

The 'deeds of chivalry and courtly manners' that a 'squire' (p. 463; 'donzel', 5) like Federigo was wont to perform were also a thing of the past in Trecento Florence. But in marrying Federigo degli Alberighi to Monna Giovanna (a woman who negotiates her way with great skill between the conflicting claims of husband, lover and son), Filomena's narrative celebrates a new social order: the marriage of courtly love, with its noble and unworldly ideals (and adulterous passions), to a more realistic valuation of wealth, property and inheritance. Such is the Florentine contribution to the narratives of love that end in 'a state of happiness'.

Dioneo tells a tale of two households: each contains a passionate wife; the first contains a conventional husband and the second a homosexual one. It would seem that the first household stands a better chance of preserving internal equilibrium than the second. But the first household breaks up in violence and confusion when the husband discovers the wife's lover hiding under the stairs (41; p. 475). The same thing happens in the second household: the wife takes a lover and the husband finds out. But in this second instance harmony is preserved as the homosexual husband institutes a new domestic order: the lover will serve both husband and wife 'to the mutual satisfaction of all three parties' (63; p. 478). This, then, is a typical Dioneo-like commentary on the themes of love, romance and social negotiation that have emerged in the course of the fifth day.

Sixth day: Florentine society and associational form

The love narratives of the fourth and fifth days have led us over huge expanses of territory and crossed many kinds of cultural and political boundaries. During the sixth day, by contrast, we never stray more than twenty miles from Florence. All of these narratives are set in the recent past (the last half-century) and most feature protagonists that are well known to the *brigata* and to Boccaccio's first audience. The theme chosen to mark this Florentine homecoming is the exercise of language under pressure: the exchange of 'like for like' by those provoked by 'some verbal pleasantry' ('leggiadro motto'), or the use of 'prompt retort or shrewd manoeuvre' by those seeking to avoid 'danger, discomfort or ridicule' ('perdita o pericolo o scorno'). Such adroit use of language was essential for the well-being of the Florentine Republic, a regime which (we have noted) took pride in its associative or laterally extending forms of polity (as opposed to the unitary, downward-descending model of power ruled over by despots and tyrannical *signori* elsewhere in Italy).

The sixth day pays particular attention to the ways in which people work together as a group in the pursuit of common interests; this includes a closer analysis of the inner dynamics of Boccaccio's *brigata*. It also explores ways in which a *brigata* may be exploited for selfish motives, and how an individual (a woman, or a solitary man) may be oppressed by group or social pressures. Boccaccio's interest in social cooperation (and its relation to individual freedom) should not be taken as a plea for democracy: although there is an effort to cooperate *within* groups, considerable distances are established *between* one kind of group and another. This becomes dramatically evident as the *brigata* gathers itself for the day's storytelling: the circle of storytellers is suddenly distracted by 'a great commotion [romore], issuing from the kitchen, among the maids and men-servants' (4; p. 480). Licisca and Tindaro, a maid and a man-servant, have been arguing whether or not Sicofante's wife was a virgin on her wedding night. Tindaro tries to speak, but Licisca cuts him short: 'you ignorant lout, how can you dare to speak first when I am present? Hold your tongue and let me tell the story' (7; p. 482). She then roundly denounces the foolishness of men who imagine that young girls will be sexually inactive as they wait for their brothers and fathers to marry them off. This leaves the women of the *brigata* helpless with laughter ('you could have pulled all their teeth out'). Elissa, queen for the Day, fails to halt this diatribe and turns the case over to Dioneo. When Dioneo pronounces Licisca to be right and Tindaro to be a fool Licisca gloats and starts speaking again. The queen now reasserts her authority by silencing Licisca, threatening her with a whipping and sending her back to the kitchen.

Although this downstairs rebellion is of short duration, it has important long-term effects upon the *Decameron*'s storytelling. In speaking of married women, Licisca asserts: 'I could tell you a thing or two about the tricks they play on their husbands'. This suggestion is taken up by Dioneo at the end of the sixth day and is adopted as the seventh day's theme. But there is no question of Licisca returning to tell her 'thing or two': she is not heard from again. Tindaro is summoned at the end of the day, but only to play his bagpipe as an accompaniment to the *brigata*'s dancing. The *brigata* will draw much of its storytelling material from the lower orders of society in the second half of the *Decameron*, but the lower orders will not be called upon to speak for themselves.

Licisca's unceremonious interruption of Tindaro ('Lascia dir me') forms something of a counter-exemplum to the first *novella*. This opens with a group of knights and ladies (much like the *Decameron*'s own *brigata*) walking through the Florentine *contado* or countryside. One of these 'knights' ('cavalieri', 6) offers to entertain one of the ladies with a story: 'Madonna Oretta, if you like I shall take you riding along a goodly stretch of our journey by telling you one of the finest tales in the world' (7; p. 484). Oretta agrees and the knight begins his tale. But he makes such an excruciating mess of it that Oretta sweats, feels faint and eventually thinks she is going to die: he repeats the same phrases and incidents, muddles his characters, apologizes for his mistakes in mid-tale and has no sense of narrative style or decorum. The problem for Oretta here, if she is to bring about a courteous imposition of silence ('un cortese impor di silenzio', 4) is not primarily one of social class: she is the man's social peer, and probably his superior since the historical Oretta Malaspina was the daughter of a marquis. The problem here is gender. A woman cannot cut short a knight's lengthy and inept narration without cutting at his exercise of manhood: lengthy discourses ('il molto parlare', 2) are (so the opening of this *novella* tells us) something that men are supposed to be good at. Oretta shows great ingenuity by developing and appearing to complete the logic of the man's own horse-back metaphor: 'Sir, you have taken me riding on a horse that trots very jerkily. Pray be good enough to set me down' (p. 484). The exquisite beauty of her formulation, with its complex metrical patternings and parallelisms, its assonances and alliteration, its delicate positioning of pronouns, is also highly suggestive of poetic closure: 'Messer, questo vostro cavallo ha troppo duro trotto, per che io vi priego che vi piaccia di pormi a piè' (11).

Oretta's need to silence a deficient speaker issues not from boredom but from acute physical distress. Competent storytelling was thought to exercise a vital hygienic function in purging social malaise; incompetence might help incubate the disease. The *brigata* is actually subjected to an incompetent *novella* by one of its own members later in the day: Emilia has been day-dreaming rather than thinking out her own storytelling. She apologizes for telling a tale 'much shorter perhaps than the one I would have told you if I had had all my wits about me' (8, 4; p. 501). Although her tale is indeed very short (only I, 9 is shorter), it still manages to replicate many of the errors attributed to the incompetent knight in the first *novella*. The tale is devoid of all context-ualizing detail (it is not clear where or when it takes place) and the 'amusing remark' it delivers up is not very amusing and (more importantly) has no effect: the female protagonist is as witless and vain 'to this day' as she was at the story's beginning. Emilia's neglect of the *brigata* (she admits that her spirit is not really here, 'qui', 4) means that the other storytellers must work the harder to keep their communal project alive.

The second *novella* begins with Pampinea questioning the wisdom of Fortune and Nature: why do they sometimes assign a noble spirit to an inferior body or an inferior social calling? Variations of this question surface throughout the *Decameron*: the Cimone story opens with an uncouth spirit in a noble body, and the *novella* featuring Giotto plays with the paradox of an artistic genius, unrivalled in his representation of Nature, being assigned by Nature to a body 'of monstrously ugly appearance' (VI, 5, 3; p. 493). But Pampinea insists that any impulse to curse Fortune and Nature should be resisted, since both of these powers show great wisdom in 'burying their most precious possessions in the least imposing (and therefore least suspect) part of their houses, whence they bring them forth in the hour of greatest need' (5; p. 485). Here, then, is an attempt to develop the notion of an intelligence buried deep within the Florentine body politic that will make itself heard at times of danger. In Pampinea's *novella* this intelligence is embodied by the unlikely figure of 'Cisti fornaio', Cisti the baker.

The *novella* is set in 1300, the year in which a papal delegation visited Florence (while Dante was serving as prior) to make peace between two feuding factions, the Black and White Guelfs. Pope Boniface's representatives, who assumed the role of peace-makers, were in fact working to bring the pro-papal Blacks to power by exterminating the Whites. This is precisely what was to happen in November 1301, when Boniface turned to Charles de Valois and his army: the Whites were massacred or (like Dante) exiled and the Blacks came to power. This, then, is the 'hour of greatest need' established by the opening of the *novella* as Cisti watches the papal ambassadors criss-crossing the city in the company of Messer Geri Spina, a prominent Florentine politician (and the husband of Madonna Oretta). Cisti needs to communicate with Messer Geri: he must make this Florentine leader recognize the character of his fellow citizens rather than devoting all his attention to the agents of the Pope. At the same time Cisti is mindful of 'the difference in rank [condizione] between himself and Messer Geri' that makes such communication a delicate business (10; p. 486). Cisti shows extraordinary ingenuity in devising a series of stratagems and signals which enable him to communicate with Messer Geri and establish a lasting friendship; at the same time, from beginning to end, he insists upon the punctilious observation of social difference.

The fourth *novella* also records an association, albeit a

momentary one, between two men of different rank. The protagonists here are Currado Gianfigliazzi, a well-known
Florentine politician from a prosperous banking family, and
Chichibio, his Venetian cook. Currado goes hunting, kills a
crane with one of his falcons and sends his catch to Chichibio.
Since Currado's crane (like Federigo's falcon) symbolizes
aristocratic pretensions it would obviously be dangerous to
abuse it. But once the bird is roasting in the kitchen it
becomes the object of desire in a new pseudo-courtly *caccia*
or hunt: Donna Brunetta, Chichibio's beloved, wants to eat
one of its legs. Chichibio is caught between the love of his
lady and loyalty to his lord. Finally love wins out, and
Chichibio is left to explain why Currado's crane has only one
leg. When Chichibio insists that *all* cranes have just the one
leg Currado is furious and insists on a field-trip to test this
hypothesis. As they approach the cranes at the riverbank,
Currado is still furious and Chichibio is witless with terror:
but suddenly, 'in some mysterious way, he thought of an
answer' (18; p. 493). This answer so delights Currado that 'all
his anger was converted [convertì] into jollity and laughter'.
The use of the verb *convertire* reminds us of Currado's banking background: Chichibio's answer finally offers him a fair
exchange for the loss of the crane's leg. The servant saves
himself by providing his master with an immediate gift of
laughter and with future social currency, a story that he can
dine out on for months to come.

This theme of social exchange dominates the third *novella*,
which begins with a husband selling one night of sex with his
wife to Messer Diego della Ratta, a Catalan nobleman currently employed as Marshal to King Robert of Naples. The
price for this is five hundred gold florins, but the Marshal
pays only five hundred *popolini*, a silver coin that was the
same size as the florin but of little value. The woman, identified only as the niece of the brother of the Bishop of
Florence, plays no further part in the story: but both male
and female Florentines are mindful of her fate; the story
becomes common knowledge. The Bishop feigns ignorance of
the whole affair and continues to ride around Florence in the

company of the Marshal. One day, however, he taunts another young woman by asking her (as he claps his hand on the Marshal's shoulder) whether she would like to make a sexual conquest of this nobleman. The woman, Monna Nonna de' Pulci, replies that if there were to be such a conquest 'I should want to be paid in good coin' (10; p. 490). This remark stings both men to the quick; they ride away 'silent and shamefaced, and said no more to Monna Nonna that day' (p. 490).

Lauretta began this *novella* by observing that there are times when words must bite like a dog rather than nibble like a sheep (3; p. 489). Monna Nonna bites like a dog because Florentine women have no other form of redress against this seedy collusion of masculine powers, an alliance of religious, political and domestic authorities (Bishop, Marshal, and husband). But it is clear that her remark is efficacious for the public world in which it is spoken: for without the stability of both coinage and marriage the Republic could not survive. (Dante, we have noted, puts master Adam, the counterfeiter of Florentine coinage, in one of the deepest pits of hell – *Inferno* XXX.) It also suggests (like the Cisti story) that Florentine leaders should think more of the interests of Florentines and be less intimate with the representatives of foreign powers.

The seventh *novella* further explores ways in which women may assert their right to independent existence in a man-made world. The man-made law that traps Madonna Filippa is a statute of Prato, her native city, requiring that women taken in adultery by their husbands be burned alive. Madonna Filippa is caught with her lover in her own bedchamber. Rinaldo, the outraged husband, can scarcely resist murdering both of them on the spot (and hence making Filippa a Francesca da Rimini figure): but he decides, instead, to secure his wife's death by sending her to the law court. Refusing either to deny her guilt or to flee the city, Filippa delivers a bold two-pronged defence of her conduct in the court of law. Her first argument elaborates the famous legal maxim *quod omnes tangit ab omnibus approbari debet*: 'laws must have the consent of those who are affected by them' (13; p. 500). When the law prescribing burning for women taken in adultery was formulated 'no woman gave her consent to it, nor was any woman even so much as consulted'. Her second argument moves from the logic of law to that of commerce and sexuality: if her husband has always taken 'as much of me as he needed', then (she asks the *podestà*) 'what am I to do with the surplus?' Her interrogation of the law delights all the citizens of Prato who have packed into the court-house, and they amend the statute on the spot. The lines of argument Madonna Filippa employs in her own defence are later re-traced by Chaucer's Wife of Bath. The chief priority for both women is the control of domestic space, the one political space which affords women a measure of self-determination. Madonna Filippa's triumph is not complete until she returns to *her* house ('la sua casa', 19), the place which her husband sought to redefine (in the public world) as the site of her crime.

Boccaccio's ninth *novella* begins by praising the masculine societies or *brigate* that used to meet in Florence to entertain themselves, their fellow citizens and foreign visitors. But it ends by celebrating a male protagonist (rather than a female one) who defies the pressures of such masculine groupings and insists on the right to keep his own company. This protagonist, Guido Cavalcanti (the great lyric poet who was thought to be an atheist), is first seen taking 'a favourite walk of his' through the ancient Roman sarcophagi that once surrounded the famous baptistry of San Giovanni (10; p. 504). His private pleasure is interrupted by members of a Florentine *brigata* who are resentful of the fact that Guido will not join their group. These men, riding on horseback, mount a mock attack on Guido and taunt him by saying: 'Guido, you spurn our company; but supposing you find that God doesn't exist, what good will it do you?' (11; p. 504). Guido gives an enigmatic reply that seems meaningless and leaves them staring at one another; meanwhile he vaults over a tomb and continues on his way.

The *brigata* eventually discovers someone in its own midst

who can explain Guido's words. This glossator, Messer Betto Brunelleschi (the addressee of Dante's *Rime* XCIX), is henceforth regarded as 'a paragon of shrewdness and intelligence': if the *brigata* cannot have Guido, they can at least recognize the talent they already possess. This celebration of the glossator with which the *novella* concludes reminds us that Boccaccio was chiefly celebrated (and sought after) in Florence as an interpreter of difficult texts. It also suggests that we might read the entire *novella* as a giant gloss on the representation of Guido in Dante's *Commedia*. Guido appears only as an absence in *Inferno* X, evoked in a conversation among the tombs where his father lies buried among other heretic Epicureans who deny the immortality of the soul. Boccaccio rehabilitates Guido by representing him as a historical protagonist (walking in the environs of San Giovanni, the epicentre of the Florence Dante longs for in exile). The *novella*'s tombs recall the landscape of *Inferno* X, and the *brigata* members recall the impudent devils of Dante's Malebolge ('Let's go and torment him', 10; p. 504). Boccaccio's account of Guido begins with a defence of his Epicureanism and ends with Guido leaping the tomb and escaping his persecutors. Perhaps these persecutors include Dante: Guido escapes from the totalizing universe of the *Commedia* to the pages of a new text, the *Decameron*, which celebrates rather than condemns his solitary and singular identity.

Although Boccaccio differs from Dante in his representation of Guido, his narrative strategy in the sixth day invites comparisons with the *Commedia* because it concentrates on Florentine protagonists of recent times: some are still living, some are dead and some (like Monna Nonna de' Pulci) have just perished in the plague. Most Florentines in Dante appear in the *Inferno*, many of them within Dis, the corrupted city that bears more than a passing resemblance to Trecento Florence. Many of the ways in which Florentines exploit language for personal profit in the sixth day are damnable by Dantean standards. But although complaints are voiced periodically about the avarice and greed of modern times, the

Decameron is undoubtedly energized by the self-serving animation of its great talkers. Two of these are heard from in the sixth day: Michele Scalza (VI, 6) and Frate Cipolla (VI, 10).

Scalza, a Florentine famed for coming up with the most bizarre *novelle* ('le più nuove novelle', 4; p. 496), actually has little to say: all he has to offer is the solution to a riddle of how own devising. His skill lies in exploiting the *brigata* structure to stage a debating competition that will win a free supper for himself and six companions. A good *novella* was obviously a prized commodity in Trecento Florence, and like any other commodity its value could rise and fall in a free market of surplus and scarcity: by the time Pampinea comes to narrate the ninth *novella*, at least two of her stories have already been told and she must draw upon one she has kept 'in reserve' (3; p. 503). Scalza could obviously deliver his one-liner without setting up such an elaborate framework for its delivery: but he knows that by delaying his narrating he will sharpen the desire for gratification in his fellow Florentines. And the subject of his riddle ('Why are the Baronci' – a well-known family of middling rank – 'the noblest of Florentine families?') will pique the interest of a society that is obsessed with the subject of nobility.

When Dioneo comes to tell the last story, he is aware that most of the sixth day's *novelle* have been exceptionally short. He needs to exercise the rhetorical skill of *amplificatio* and spin out a longer narrative, and so he turns to a professional spinner-out of words, Frate Cipolla. Cipolla (whose name means 'onion': he is a man of many layers) is a friar, a member of a dynamic new international group of professional religious whose rise accompanied that of the international market economy in the later Middle Ages. Whereas Benedictine monks were content to remain in their rural monasteries (meeting the educational and religious needs of the landed aristocracy), the friars were dedicated to serving the new urban world (and to skimming off a share of the new urban wealth). In Dioneo's *novella*, the friar Cipolla has come to the country town of Certaldo, where people still followed 'the honest precepts of an earlier age': an age that knows nothing of 'the luxuries of Egypt' which have now flooded the market, 'to the ruination of the whole of Italy' (27; p. 509). Cipolla's mission is to collect dues from the confraternity of Saint Anthony and to show them 'a most sacred and beautiful relic' (11; p. 507): one of the feathers of the Archangel Gabriel (dropped in the Virgin Mary's bedchamber at the time of the Annunciation). The honest country-folk seem helpless against the seamless rhetoric ('he was Cicero in person, or perhaps Quintillian', 7; p. 506) of the urbane friar: but two young men even the odds by exchanging the feather for a lump of coal. And yet when Cipolla discovers this exchange, in mid-sermon, he simply changes his story: this is a lump of coal from the fire over which St Lawrence was griddled. When the sermon ends the Certaldese give 'larger offerings than usual'; Cipolla takes the coal and scrawls 'the biggest crosses he could manage to inscribe on their white smocks and on their doublets and on the shawls of the women' (54; p. 513).

At the very end of the *novella* the two young men (having 'laughed until they thought their sides would split') meet with Cipolla, explain the substitution and hand back his feather. They are identified not as members of the religious confraternity, but rather as members of Cipolla's *brigata* ('di sua brigata', 13; p. 502). The narrative economy of the entire *novella* is a closed circle; the hapless rural confraternity is a blank page for Cipolla to write on. Boccaccio himself, of course, comes from Certaldo: but his sixth day narratives put him in Frate Cipolla's *brigata* rather than with those who dream of 'the honest precepts of an earlier age'.

Seventh day: controlling domestic space

At the end of the sixth day the *brigata* becomes more clearly divided along gender lines than at any earlier point. Some of the women are not keen to debate the topic Dioneo has chosen for the seventh day (the tricks women have played upon their husbands) but Dioneo enforces his choice by

appealing to his authority as monarch-for-the-day. As soon
as Dioneo becomes absorbed in a game of dice with the other
men, Elissa draws the women together and takes them to a
secret place called the Valley of the Ladies. Here they bathe
in a limpid pool 'which concealed their chaste white bodies no
better than a thin sheet of glass would conceal a pink rose'
(conclusion 30; p. 517). They then return to the dice-players
and tell them how they have been deceived ('ingannati', 33).
Dioneo then gathers the men and their servants together and,
having deserted the ladies ('lasciate le donne', 36), they make
their own trip to the Valley. They find the place so enchanting
that Dioneo decides to move the *brigata* there for the seventh
day. The servants move out early next morning with a large
baggage train; the *brigata* follows and the Valley of the
Ladies becomes the new site for the storytelling.

The first and seventh stories of the sixth day showed how
gender difference shades into political difference; the
Madonna Filippa narrative teaches that a medieval woman's
first priority is control of her own household. All nine of the
seventh day narratives of gender conflict (Dioneo departs
from the theme he prescribes) concentrate on this battle for
the control of domestic space. This is best described as a
political conflict since, in the words of Aristotle, the thinker
who exerted most influence on medieval political thought, the
household is the primary unit of political life: 'the state is
made up of households' (*Politics* 1253 b 1). Ideally speaking,
of course, the household was the place where men and women
lived out the sacrament of marriage, the mystery which makes
one flesh of two genders. But it was also the site of an alliance
between two family networks that were sensitive to the
minutest gradations of social status. When a Florentine
woman married, she brought a dowry with her that symbolized the status of the donor family: but as she took her husband's name, this dowry passed to his control and could not
easily be recovered even in the event of his death. It was
important, then, for a wife to control domestic space because
all her hopes for present and future prosperity and status were
irretrievably invested in it. The women of the seventh day

demonstrate an extraordinary range of stratagems for securing or recovering such control; three winning formulas are
offered by the fourth, fifth and sixth *novelle*, set in the mid-
peninsula cities of Arezzo, Rimini, and Florence.

The fourth *novella* presents us with a worst-case scenario:
a woman locked out in the street by a husband threatening to
expose her infidelity 'in front of your kinsfolk and
neighbours' (12; p. 539). This, for the heroine Monna Ghita,
would amount to social death: and so she makes a threat of
equivalent force by laying down her distaff (the symbol of
wifely authority) and proposing to commit suicide by jump-
ing down a well. The husband, Tofano, is unimpressed until
he hears a large plopping sound. He then rushes out of the
house; Monna Ghita rushes in and bolts the door (the plop
having been made by a large stone.) Their positions are now
reversed and Monna Ghita is happy to carry on a shouting
match with her husband that brings her neighbours running.
She knows that the most powerful argument is the one that
comes from the house: 'You see the sort of man he is! What
would you say if I were in the street and he was in the house,
instead of the other way round?' (26; p. 541). Tofano is
discredited; word spreads to her kinsfolk and they beat him
black and blue. Ghita returns to live with her own family until
her husband sues for peace and agrees to let her wander at her
leisure in the future. The wife wins control of her own front
door.

In the fifth *novella* a wife experiences difficulty not in getting into the house but in getting out of it. A young wife
(Fiammetta tells us) needs to enjoy herself on Sundays after
a week of labour, looking after her house and family, 'just as
farm-labourers do, or the workers in the towns, or the
magistrates on the bench' (4; p. 542). But the jealous husband
in this *novella* will not let his wife so much as stand at the window. This drives the wife to hunt through the house from top
to bottom in search of a crack or fissure that will enable her
to communicate with the outside world. Finally, 'in a very
remote part of the house' (13; p. 544), she discovers a crack
in the wall adjoining the bedroom of the young man next

door. She attracts his attention by dropping pieces of stone and straw through the crack. He widens the hole on his side and finally their hands touch. This ingenious urban updating of the Pyramus and Thisbe story completes the first part of the plot.

The second narrative sequence opens with the wife finally leaving the house for the only private activity she is allowed to pursue outside her own doors: confession in church. The husband (the protagonists are not named) is jealous and suspicious that his wife should have anything to confess (since he keeps her locked in the house all day). He bribes the chaplain, wears a hood, puts gravel in his mouth to alter his voice and plays the part of confessor to his own wife. The wife (who recognizes him immediately) confesses to sleeping with a priest who enters her front door every night and takes her husband's place. The husband-priest is mortified and resolves to sit up all night to intercept this intruder. He pretends to have a supper engagement and instructs his wife to seal off all segments of the house: 'take good care to lock the front door, the landing door, and the bedroom door' (38; p. 547). He then sits waiting for the intruder, 'supperless, aching all over, and freezing to death'. The young lover picks his way over the rooftop and enters the wife's bedroom window; they make love all night, secure in the knowledge that the door is locked against the husband by the husband's own instructions. This goes on night after night until the wife finally enlightens the husband: *he* is the priest who enters her bed and takes her husband's place. The husband now looks at his wife as 'a model of intelligence and virtue' (59; p. 549); he is completely cured of his jealousy just at the point when 'his need for it was paramount'. The wife is now free to enjoy herself: from that day forward she 'no longer admitted her lover by way of the roof as though he were some kind of cat, but showed him in at the front door' (59; p. 550).

In the fourth *novella* the house is a haven; in the fifth it is a prison; in the sixth it becomes a highway, with the wife directing the traffic. Madonna Isabella, convinced that her husband is out of the picture for a few days, welcomes her lover into the bedroom of her country villa. But then a second suitor arrives; the first is hurriedly hidden behind the curtains. The second lover enters the bedroom: but then the husband arrives home. Things look grim: 'finding herself with two men in the house, and knowing that it was impossible to conceal the second because his horse was standing in the yard, the lady thought her hour had come' (15; p. 552). But Isabella, suddenly inspired, finds a brilliant and dramatic solution for her dilemma. The second suitor leaves on his own horse; the first is escorted by her husband 'to his own front door' (29; p. 554).

Our sense that these narratives add up to a primer or courtesy book for urban women is encouraged by the first *novella*, which adopts a mock-pedagogical style and promises to teach 'something that might prove useful to you [women] in the future'. It emerges at the end of the *novella* that the 'fine and godly prayer' Emilia proposes to teach exists in two variant versions; and that there are different accounts of how the ass's skull on the vine stake (a crucial narrative signal) came to face in the wrong direction at the crucial moment. It also becomes evident that just as men learn from their masculine teachers (the husband Gianni is kept away from his house by the friars of Santa Maria Novella who teach him 'the song of Saint Alexis and the lament of Saint Bernard and the laud of Lady Matilda and a whole lot of other drivel', 5; p. 523), so women learn from their female ones: the 'godly prayer' that keeps the husband from the bedroom while the wife is busy with her lover is taught by a hermitess ('the most saintly woman you ever met', 23; p. 525); the riddle of the variant versions of the prayer and the skull-turning is solved by a female exegete who pops up from nowhere at the end of the narrative ('there is a neighbour of mine, a very old woman, who tells me . . .' 33; p. 527).

The suggestion or suspicion that women control their households through some kind of magic persists throughout the day, although it is clear that it is the very suspicion of female magic that prevents husbands from seeing what is really going on; their wives are invariably rational and business-like. A male magician appears in the third *novella*, but his magic evaporates once he takes his clothes off. When he is caught in bed with another man's wife his nakedness robs him of his power: 'If only I had my clothes on', he says, 'we could invent some explanation' (26; p. 535). This man is both a friar and a godparent to the woman's child; friars and godfathers feature quite prominently in the seventh day because they have privileged access to wives alone in their houses. The friar in the third *novella* knows that his magic lies in his habit; once the wife has bought him time and given him the clue for a solution he can dress himself and exercise his craft by pretending to charm worms from his godchild. The poor husband is, of course, powerless to resist this combination of wifely and friarly magic; he weeps with joy to see that his child has been snatched from the grave and treats everyone to wine and sweetmeats.

Some of the ways that wives find to deceive their husbands climax in real virtuoso performances. Peronella's husband, in the second *novella*, ends up inside a giant wine tub, scraping away with his tool, convinced that his wife has found a buyer for the tub (once it is cleaned). Peronella leans over the tub, directing scraping operations with a stream of instructions. The prospective buyer, meanwhile, is working away at Peronella from the rear. When all the scraping is done the buyer pays the husband seven silver ducats for the tub and (inevitably) gets him 'to carry it round to his house' (36; p. 531). In the seventh *novella* a lady in her darkened bedroom grips her lover's hand, wakes up her husband and tells of the lover's betrayal (he is one of her husband's most trusted servants); she then persuades the husband to dress up in her clothes and leave the house while she makes love to the servant in the husband's bed.

What is it that drives women to such extremes of ingenuity and danger? The narrator of the fourth *novella* begins with a long paean to Love; only Love could teach such wisdom, insights and subterfuges (3–4; p. 538). Such rhetoric seemed appropriate as part of the great love narratives of the fourth and fifth days, but it is oddly out of place here in introducing the short urban farce of this fourth *novella*; its effect is ironic. Wives in the seventh day take lovers not because Love wills it, but because they need to exercise their own powers of self-determination. In the fourth and fifth *novelle* wives rebel against husbands who restrict their freedom of movement (the husband in VII, 5 is identified only as 'il geloso', 'Master Jealous'); in the sixth Madonna Isabella simply fancies 'a change of diet' (5; p. 550). Their restlessness only mirrors that of their male counterparts in a restless and dynamic society: the father and son in the seventh *novella* pass through four different social degrees in three different locales in the space of seven pages (nobleman, merchant, squire, servant; Florence, France, Bologna). Women cannot choose to make such dramatic changes of place or social station in the public world; the greatest exercise of self-determination open to them is a change of lover in their own house.

The eighth and ninth *novelle* bring all the plots, themes, and issues of the seventh day to new levels of intensity and complication. The eighth *novella* boasts perhaps the most extraordinary go-between device ever invented: a wife, in bed with her husband, communicates with her lover in the street below by means of a string tied to her big toe. The husband, a rich merchant, has been bound for disaster ever since he 'foolishly decided to marry into the aristocracy' (4; p. 561). Once he discovers the toe-string device the merchant-husband is sure that he can prove his wife's infidelity and get her relatives to remove her as damaged goods: 'you're certainly not going to stay in this house any longer' (21; p. 563). But his aristocratic wife outsmarts him and reduces him to a state of open-mouthed silence. This allows the wife's mother to launch a furious tirade against the pretensions of the *nuova gente*: 'To hell with this small-time trader in horse manure! . . . These country yokels, they move into town after serving as cut-throat to some petty rustic tyrant, and wander about the streets in rags and tatters, their trousers all askew, with a quill sticking out from their backsides [colla penna in culo], and no sooner do they get a few pence in their pockets than they want the daughters of noble gentlemen and fine ladies for their wives' (46; p. 567). At the end of the *novella* the merchant-husband is still gazing vacantly into space, 'not knowing whether the things he had done were real or part of a dream' (50; p. 568).

In the ninth *novella* Boccaccio turns (once again) to an ancient and classical setting in order to develop a narrative that has the originary and explanatory power of myth: in this case, a narrative that shows how a wife so dominates and entrances her husband that he comes to doubt the evidence of his own senses. The story is taken from the *Comedia Lydiae* once attributed to Matthew of Vendome, a Latin poem that Boccaccio had copied into one of his *zibaldoni* (literary miscellanies) some years earlier; this *novella* provides one of the few occasions in the *Decameron* in which Boccaccio may be observed working closely from a specific literary source. In the first part of the narrative Lydia, wife of the Greek patrician Nicostratos, proves to her lover, Pyrrhus, that she has total control of her spouse and her household: she kills her husband's favourite hawk at a public banquet; she rips out a tuft of his beard; she yanks out one of his teeth. Predictably enough, Nicostratos (who has been persuaded that one of his teeth, which is perfectly healthy, is rotten) persuades himself that he feels 'much better' once Lydia has gone to work with the pincers (55; p. 575). Having met these three challenges, put to her by her lover, Lydia adds a challenge of her own: she will make love to Pyrrhus in full view of her husband and persuade her husband that what he is seeing is not true ('che ciò non fosse vero'). To achieve this Lydia leaves the house (which she now dominates) and enters the garden, the primeval site of both love-making and myth-making. Here she makes love and (with the aid of a supposedly magical pear tree) establishes the myth taken up by Chaucer's *Merchant's Tale*: that even when a husband sees what his wife is doing, his wife will find words to persuade him that his vision is faulty.

Eighth day: the scholar and the widow

When Lauretta succeeds Dioneo as monarch-for-the-day she

rejects the obvious choice of subject matter: rather than just throwing the seventh day into reverse and telling of the tricks men play on their wives, the *brigata* is to consider 'the tricks that people in general, men and women alike, are forever playing on each other' (conclusion, 4; p. 583). Translated more pedantically, the formula is 'the tricks [beffe] that are forever being played either by woman on man or by man on woman or by one man on another'. The missing combination here, of course, is woman on woman: there are no narratives of female enmity in the *Decameron*, and none of female friendship either. Stories of masculine friendship form an important element, but Boccaccio's text gives no sign of recognizing that there could be such a thing as a *novella* featuring two female protagonists and no men.

The mercantile society of Trecento Florence frequently expressed the stresses and strains generated by its own volatile and expansionist energies through narratives of gender conflict. Giovanni Villani's chronicle records as fact some historical phenomena that are more fantastic than any Boccaccian fiction. In writing of the marvellous signs that accompanied the plague year of 1347, for example, he tells of a territory under the Sultan in which all the men died: only women were left, but without the restraining influence of men they became so enraged that they ate one another (IV, 133). Villani (a merchant who married above his station) was an enthusiastic supporter of sumptuary laws (dress codes for women) and maintained that it was women's demand for ever more extravagant forms of dress and ornament that drove their merchant husbands ever further from home.

The first and last *novelle* of the *Decameron*'s eighth day show women entering into (if not originating) the spirit of the market economy. In the first story a German soldier at Milan called Gulfardo falls in love with Madonna Ambruogia, the wife of a wealthy merchant. Gulfardo sends a message to Ambruogia, begging her to grant him 'the sweet reward of his devotion' (p. 588). She replies that she would be pleased to do so: the price is two hundred gold florins. Gulfardo is 'incensed at her lack of decorum'; his love turns to hate and he determines to trick her ('di doverla beffare', 8). He borrows two hundred gold florins from Guasparruolo, the merchant husband, at 'the same rate of interest as usual'; when Guasparruolo has gone on a business trip he pays them to his wife. Ambruogia and Gulfardo then make love several times before the husband returns home. Gulfardo subsequently tells Guasparruolo that since he did not need the florins after all he handed them back to his wife. Ambruogia is thereby forced to hand back 'the ill-gotten proceeds of her depravity' to her husband; the 'sagacious lover' has had 'his rapacious lady free of charge' (18; p. 590).

In beginning this narrative, Neifile insists that women must maintain an absolute distinction between Love and trade: 'any woman who strays from the path of virtue for monetary gain deserves to be burnt alive' (3; p. 588). But it is not easy to observe such a distinction in a world in which all relationships are established 'per prezzo', 'for monetary gain'. Gulfardo, for example, is a mercenary soldier, a man who fights on short-term contracts and switches allegiances when he can command a higher price. Guasparruolo is just one of many merchants who make loans to mercenaries when they need to purchase armour and equipment. Usury was forbidden by the Church (theologians argued that the lending of money at interest amounted to the selling of time, and that time belonged to God alone) but had become indispensable for the expanding market economy. Milan was the centre of the European arms trade: hundreds of workshops forged armour and weaponry for armies and mercenaries to buy; merchants hurried to battlefields and bought up surplus stock at bargain prices once the battle was won or lost. Ambruogia, whose name recalls Ambrogio (Ambrose), Milan's most famous saint, is obviously a representative figure: she represents the crass commercialism and rapacious self-interest of the Lombard city. But rather than condemning the whole city, Boccaccio's narrative is content to denounce a single woman. The suggestion is thereby implanted that rather than just *representing* self-interested commercialism woman is the *cause* of it.

This short narrative lacks the humour of Chaucer's *Ship-man's Tale*, a more elaborate version of the same story. But Chaucer's grasp of the details of commodity exchange and credit financing (Chaucer worked in the London customs house) is matched by the tenth *novella*, which begins with a detailed description of the *dogana* (customs) system as found 'in the seaports of all maritime countries' (4; p. 666). The tale unfolds at Palermo, where a certain class of women, 'lovely of body but hostile of virtue', wait for foreign merchants to register their wares; they then read the *dogana* register to see what they have in stock, take the merchants to bed and set about 'skinning them wholesale' (7–8; p. 667). The tale then further narrows its focus by concentrating on the battle of wits between one Sicilian woman and one Florentine merchant. Deceptions and counter-deceptions become so elaborate that the reader needs an atlas and an abacus to keep track of things: 'I am utterly ruined' (the merchant tells the female con-artist)

for the ship carrying the goods I was expecting has been seized by Monegasque pirates. They are demanding a ransom of ten thousand gold florins, of which I have to pay a thousand, and I haven't a penny to my name, because as soon as you paid me back those five hundred florins, I sent them to Naples to be invested in a consignment of linen which is now on its way to Palermo. . .   (57–8; p. 676).

At the end of the narrative the Florentine retires from commerce and moves to Ferrara; the lady is left to mourn her financial losses with a jingle repeated by Florentine writers from Sacchetti to Poliziano: 'Chi ha a far con tosco, non vuole esser losco' ('Honesty's the better line, when dealing with a Florentine', 67; p. 678).

The seventh *novella*, the most powerful and arresting narrative of the eighth day, seems, at first glance, to eschew this new commercial world by returning us to a more ancient tradition of gender conflict, namely clerical anti-feminism. But this long-lived anti-feminist tradition did not disappear with the emergence of the international market economy. Nor was it displaced by the newly emergent humanist movement. The first humanists, specifically Boccaccio and

Petrarch, never thought of themselves as leading a revolt against established religious values or clerical traditions. They were, indeed, clerics as well as scholars. Any narrative that pits a scholar ('uno scolare') against a widow (a sexually experienced woman) is going to have some bearing on their identity. Perhaps this is why this seventh *novella* is the longest narrative not just of the seventh day but of the entire *Decameron*. And it was not long enough: Boccaccio felt compelled to rewrite it several years later as the *Corbaccio*, a text that contains some of the most virulent anti-feminist material ever written; it was the last vernacular fiction he ever wrote.

The length of the seventh *novella* owes little to its plot, which is relatively straightforward. Rinieri, a scholar newly returned from Paris, falls for a young Florentine widow and writes her letters in which he declares his love. The widow, who has a lover of her own choosing, is not interested: but (to entertain her lover) she decides to trick Rinieri into believing that he is to spend the night with her. Rinieri spends the night after Christmas locked in a courtyard, believing that the widow is about to admit him. Having finally realized that the lady is entertaining a lover while he is almost freezing outside, he plots his revenge. He finally traps the lady on the top of a tower, naked and with no means of descent, and leaves her to be scorched all day by the fierce July sun. The symmetry of this plot is not matched by the space allotted for its elaboration: the scholar's torment takes up one-third of the narrative and the lady's two-thirds; almost half of the *novella* is given over to the dialogue between the lady, naked on the tower, and the scholar below.

This dialogue and the conflict it forms part of fuse together many different literary strains. The widow's name is Helen (Elena); she is the only female protagonist in the *Decameron* to bear the name of the woman who inspired the disaster of ancient Troy. Rinieri also likens her to a poisonous serpent, the most ancient enemy ('antichissimo nemico') who caused mankind to be expelled from Eden (87; p. 634). But perhaps the most eloquent representation of female/male difference is that of heat and cold, a simple, elemental opposition that does not balance itself out (to form a lukewarm compromise) but remains fiercely antithetical when played out through time (July and December). Such imagery of freezing and burning leads us, of course, deep into the imaginative territory of Dante's *Inferno*: the Ugolino cantos, in particular, form a powerful sub-text to Rinieri's physical and emotional freezing and the lady's ordeal in the tower. But the language of freezing and burning also evokes a more recent strain of imagery, the torments of the Petrarchan lover.

When the scholar, freezing in the courtyard, complains to the widow that 'I scarcely have any feeling left in my body', the widow answers with a literary critique: 'You always complain in your letters that you are burning all over because of your love for me. But it's clear to me now that you must have been joking' (37; p. 626). By the end of his ordeal the scholar no longer recognizes any difference between inner, spiritual feeling and outer, physical state. Like Ugolino, frozen at the bottom of Hell, his inner feelings match the desolation of the outer landscape: 'his fervent and longstanding love was transformed into bitter and savage hatred' (40; p. 626). This transformation is accompanied by a fundamental change in his attitude to language: Ruggieri no longer employs the extravagant and paradoxical metaphors of the lover, but speaks like a philosopher whose words mean precisely what they say. His devising of the lady's punishment reflects this new determination to make literary figures, even metaphors, represent the truth. When the lady realizes that the ladder to the top of the tower has been taken away she feels 'as though the world beneath her feet had suddenly been taken away' (72; p. 632). This is, of course, just what has happened.

The widow soon realizes that she is to provide the raw material for a new kind of linguistic practice, a philosopher's *exercitatio*: 'Non voler le tue forze contro a una femina *essercitare*', she begs him (my italics: 'Don't apply your strength against a mere woman', 79; p. 633). But she immediately attempts to sway his feelings with an extravagant metaphor, thereby providing him with a perfect opportunity for exercising those skills: 'the eagle that conquers a dove has nothing to boast about'. Rinieri rejects her 'tears and honeyed [melati] words' and goes on to propose 'that you are not a dove, but a poisonous snake' (81–7; pp. 633–4). This seems, at first, no more than a substitution of terms within a metaphorical structure. But by the end of the *novella*, when the woman's skin has become so scorched and cracked that she seems to have become 'the ugliest thing in the world', Rinieri returns to his snake imagery to tell her that she will escape from her ordeal with her beauty unimpaired, 'like a snake that has sloughed off its skin' (126; p. 641).

The lengthy dialogue between the scholar and the widow may be read, then, as one of many medieval variations of the age-old debate in which the masculine figure of philosophy strips away the pretensions and disguises of the lady rhetoric. But this debate is also a discourse about a scholar's rage against real women and a renunciation of his own past devotion to them: Helen's deception is a beauty that promises to match a man's longing but that fades with time. Rinieri exposes her deception by taking command of time and accelerating the aging process: after one day in the tower the lady looks 'more like a burnt log than a human form' (140; p. 643). She is a false text; her burning skin is 'rent asunder like a piece of flaming parchment being stretched from both ends' (114; p. 639). This destruction of the old woman is accompanied by the taking of a new one: 'I have found a lady who is far more worthy of my love, and understands me better [meglio m'ha conosciuto] than you ever did' (106; p. 637).

This lady, who is never named, is presumably no lady at all but the allegorical personification Lady Philosophy. The promise of this new lady is Petrarch's *De vita solitaria*, 'Of the solitary life'. But in Boccaccio's *novella* the scholar comes to self-knowledge ('io mi conosco') only through his conflict with the lady: she taught him more in one night than he learned during all his years of studying at Paris (85; p. 634). And although he boasts of 'the power of the pen' (99; p. 636) he can think of nothing better to do with it than write about her and her kind. Such is the enabling self-contradiction of all misogynistic discourse.

Ninth day: the mystery of Calandrino

At the end of the eighth day the storytellers are released from the discipline of speaking on a prescribed theme and, like oxen unchained from the yoke, are put out to grass and allowed to wander 'wherever they please' (3; p. 679). On the ninth day each person speaks 'as he likes and on whatever subject most pleases him' (rubric). Two storytellers take this opportunity to speak of Calandrino, an anti-heroic protagonist who has already been the subject of two eighth-day *novelle*. Stories about Calandrino, Filostrato says, cannot help but 'multiplicar la festa' (IX, 3, 3; 'enhance the gaiety of our proceedings', p. 691). The 'doings [fatti] of Calandrino' are always amusing, according to Neifile; such stories promote joy and pleasure even if they have been heard a thousand times before (IX, 5, 4–5; p. 701). The Calandrino legend proliferates not only within the *Decameron*, but after the *Decameron*: Sacchetti, for example, has three *novelle* dedicated to him, and the phrase *far Calandrino* (to trick someone) becomes proverbial. Calandrino (like Shakespeare's Falstaff) is a character that exceeds his original fictional frame; audiences cannot get enough of him.

But before attempting to analyse the mysterious, singular attraction of Calandrino we should recognize that he appears in the *Decameron* within a stable complex of relationships based on historical personages and genuine Florentine locations. Filostrato makes this insistence upon historical accuracy part of the aesthetic of his storytelling (IX, 5, 5; p. 701). Mindful, then, that this *insistence* upon historicity is itself a literary effect, we can note that Calandrino was the nickname of one Giovannozzo di Perino, a painter who appears in Florentine records between 1301 and 1318. He lived in the quarter of San Lorenzo at the intersection of Via Finori and Via Guelfa; some of his frescoes survive in a villa at Camerata. Bruno and Buffalmacco, the two men that

Calandrino was most fond of ('spezializissimamente amava', VIII, 3, 26) are mentioned in an archival document of 1320 along with Giotto. Bruno di Giovanni Olivieri, like Calandrino, was a painter of middling talent, but Buffalmacco (the nickname of Bonamico, c. 1262–1340) was a talented *maestro* who left many important works in Umbria and Tuscany. He is credited with directing the famous dramatic representation of the Inferno in boats on the Arno on 1 May 1304 and he merits a *Vita* in Vasari's *Lives of the Painters*. Like Bruno, he lived on Via del Cocomero ('Melon Street') near the Mercato Vecchio. Nello (a relative of Calandrino's wife, Monna Tessa) was, or is based upon, Nello di Bandino, a painter inscribed in the *Libro della compagnia de' pittori* for the year 1306.

The first man to trick Calandrino (VIII, 3) is not a painter at all but a broker, Maso del Saggio, who was first named by Frate Cipolla as a reliable witness to the authenticity of his relics (VI, 10, 42; p. 511). What, if anything, is the social function of this *brigata* of tricksters that forms itself around Calandrino? This question is easiest answered by referring to two *novelle* in which Calandrino does not actually appear, namely VIII, 5 and VIII, 9. In VIII, 5 Maso del Saggio is sitting in a Florentine law-court when he is struck by the judge's 'curious and witless appearance' (6; p. 611). The following day, having conspired with two companions, he makes a loud appeal to the judge about a stolen pair of thigh-boots. As Maso pulls at the judge's robe from one side and one of his companions, the supposed thigh-boot thief, pulls from the other the third conspirator (hidden under the dais) pulls down the judge's breeches from below. Naked justice is suddenly revealed. The outraged judge demands to know 'whether it was the custom in Florence for a judge to have his breeches removed whilst sitting on the bench of justice' (19; p. 613). The short answer is yes: if the *podestà* (appointed from outside Florence on a short-term contract) brings half-witted justices with him, men 'who seem to have been brought up behind a plough or in a cobbler's shop' (4; p. 611), then their shortcomings will be exposed to public ridicule. The *podestà*, under advisement, wisely decides 'to hold his tongue, and nothing more was said about the matter' (20; p. 613).

In VIII, 9 a Florentine citizen, Master Simone da Villa, returns to Florence 'dressed in scarlet robes and a fine-looking hood' (5; p. 650) after studying medicine at Bologna. Having set up house in the Via del Cocomero, he is struck by the demeanour of his neighbours Bruno and Buffalmacco: 'they seemed to him the jolliest and most carefree fellows in the world' (8; p. 651). He concludes that they must be drawing 'profetti grandissimi' (8) from some secret source; only this could explain their cheerfulness in the face of apparent poverty. The two painters, who take secret pleasure in the physician's 'extraordinary simplicity' ('nuove novelle', 10), encourage him in this belief: they belong, they say, to a secret society founded by the Scottish necromancer Michael Scott; this has invested them with fabulous powers. The physician is keen to join this society and agrees to undergo a complex ritual of initiation. Buffalmacco, dressed as a devil, picks him up at the Piazza Santa Maria Novella, carries him to the westward edge of the city and finally tosses him into a sewage pit. Here the doctor, 'having parted company with his doctoral hood', swallows 'several drams of the ditchwater' (100; p. 664). The *novella* ends in moralizing vein by claiming to have shown 'how wisdom is imparted to anyone who has not acquired much of it in Bologna' (112; p. 666).

In both of these *novelle* the Florentine tricksters prove to be most adept at spotting the false pretensions of foreign credentials and in removing the pretender from the body politic. They are obviously performing a vital civic function: the Florentine judicial system depended on the competence of foreigners and many of Florence's doctors and lawyers were trained at Bologna. The moralizing prescription which ends the ninth *novella* is prompted as much by a sense of inferiority as by self-confidence: when Boccaccio wrote the *Decameron* the Florentine Studio was still struggling to establish itself, whereas Bologna boasted the oldest university in the west; it was particularly distinguished in medicine and law. Indeed, the kind of free-floating social role assigned to Boccaccio's tricksters is typically played by students in medieval narratives of French or English provenance.

Matters get more complicated when we consider how and why Boccaccio's painters go to work on Calandrino because Calandrino is one of their own: we first see him staring intently at the paintings and the new bas-reliefs (commissioned in 1313) above the high altar of San Giovanni, the famous Florentine Baptistry. This immediately presents us with the paradox of an artist entranced by art: Calandrino has no ability to detect the artificial, fictive or illusory character of anything he sees or hears. The historical Calandrino is thought to have studied with Andrea Tafi and therefore to have belonged to the school of Florentine painting that was most resistant to the visual revolution ushered in by Giotto; and Giotto, Boccaccio tells us, is so faithful to Nature 'that people's eyes are deceived and they mistake the picture for the real thing' (VI, 5, 5; p. 494). In a post-Giottesque world Calandrino is hopelessly vulnerable.

The enchantment that Calandrino experiences in art extends to all aspects of the world around him. His behaviour is affected by a charm, spell or potion in every narrative he appears in, and Maso has little trouble in persuading him in VIII, 3 that there is a special stone, the heliotrope, that will render him invisible. In the course of a field-trip to the Mugnone valley (just outside Florence), Bruno and Buffalmacco convince Calandrino that he has, indeed, discovered this stone and is now totally invisible. The spell holds good until he returns home and his wife, Monna Tessa, sees him from the top of the stairs and upbraids him for being late for breakfast. Calandrino, realizing that the spell is broken, becomes mad with rage and beats his wife black and blue. When his companions arrive to ask what all the commotion is about Calandrino has already deduced why the magic no longer works: 'all things lose their virtue (virtù) in the ppresence of a woman' (61; p. 604).

The attraction Calandrino evidently held for a Florentine audience might be read as nostalgia for a world-view of immanent mystery that was fast disappearing: the kind of charismatic power he both exemplifies and believes in recedes, according to Max Weber, as societies become more bureaucratized and more dependent upon principle of rational calculation. But Calandrino does, of course, find a rationale for the breaking of his magic, one that the scholar of VIII, 7 might endorse: virtue fails in the presence of woman. The term *virtù*, according to Cicero and the Church Fathers, is derived from the Latin *vir*, meaning man. Virtue is the essence of manliness, woman is its oppposite, and the threshold of the house that woman rules over marks the limit of all masculine magic, dreams and fantasy. This is obviously a myth of considerable longevity. The conflict between Calandrino and his wife forms an important part of the Calandrino legend and is gloriously resolved in the final *novella* (IX, 5), when Tessa avenged herself by leaving Calandrino 'scratched and torn to ribbons' (67; p. 709).

Calandrino is actually safer at home than he is abroad because Tessa, 'a handsome-looking gentlewoman' (VIII, 3, 51; p. 602), shields him from the magic the tricksters wish to work on him. But in all four narratives Calandrino experiences a strong impulse to leave the house and head for the countryside: to collect magic stones (VIII, 3); to butcher a pig (VIII, 6); to buy a farm (IX, 3); and to paint frescoes and woo a lady in a country villa (IX, 5). This gravitational pull away from the city suggests that there is something of the countryman about Calandrino: he embodies an enduring rustic simplicity and credulity against which Florentine urbanity defines and exercises itself. Business-minded urbanites always triumph over ingenuous rustics in the *Decameron*. The most extreme and one-sided victory comes in the final *novella* of the ninth day, in which a trader-priest convinces a peasant, Neighbour Pietro, that his wife can be turned into a mare by day (and so help out with business) if she kneels naked on all-fours and allows priestly magic to be worked from the rear. The trader-priest casts his spell and then convinces Pietro that he has broken the charm: Pietro was commanded to be silent, but he cried out just as the priest was sticking on the tail. Pietro's wife sides with the priest, denounces her husband and so lays down the basic law of rural poverty in the *Decameron*: 'So help me God, you're as poor as a church mouse already, but you deserve to be a lot poorer' (23; p. 730). Calandrino always ends up in Neighbour

Pietro's shoes, contemplating the abject failure of the grandiose plans that urban tricksters have seduced him with.

Calandrino is especially vulnerable in VIII, 6 because he is both out in the country and alone in the house: his wife falls sick and cannot join him on a trip to their farm to butcher a pig. When Bruno and Buffalmacco hear of this they immediately move to the countryside, get Calandrino drunk and steal his pig. They then persuade him to participate in a traditional divination exercise, 'la esperienza del pane e del formaggio': whoever has stolen the pig will be unable to swallow bread and cheese (32; p. 617). Employing ginger sweets instead of bread and cheese, they doctor two of them by using hepatic aloes and *zenzaro canino*, ginger of inferior quality. (Translators used to think the phrase 'del cane' (39) indicated that they used dog-stools, but scholarship has mercifully saved Calandrino from this fate.) The tasting scene forms a perfect rural tableau: farmworkers and Florentines on holiday gather by the elm in front of the village church to share ginger sweets and wine. Calandrino, of course, is unable to swallow the two doctored sweets, but he makes mighty efforts to do so: 'tears as big as hazel-nuts began to roll down his cheeks' (48; p. 619). Calandrino's tears reveal him as the thief; the painters charge him two brace of capons as the price for not informing Monna Tessa. They then salt his pig and return to Florence.

In IX, 3 (which must be chronologically anterior to VIII, 6), Calandrino comes into some money and decides to buy a farm. Bruno and Buffalmacco, faithful to their own principle of *carpe diem*, mock Calandrino's impulse 'to go buying land, as if he needed it to make mud pies' (5; p. 692). When he persists in his plans, they conspire with Nello and convince Calandrino that he is seriously sick. Calandrino retires to his bedroom and calls to Tessa with words that prove comically prophetic: 'come and cover me well [cuoprimi bene]; I'm feeling very poorly' (16; p. 693). The *beffa* has gone smoothly to this point, but it seems doubtful that it can proceed much further because the sensible Monna Tessa now dominates the scene. But in Calandrino narratives Calandrino himself often finds a way for the plot to move forward (even a plot against himself) when all options seem exhausted. When the doctor (the physician from VIII, 9 another co-conspirator) gives Calandrino his diagnosis ('you are pregnant') Calandrino knows just who is to blame: 'Ah, Tessa, this is your doing! You always insist on lying on top' (21; p. 694). Tessa turns red with embarrassment, lowers her gaze and leaves the room without speaking a word. This masculine victory in the fight for domestic space is a rare event in the *Decameron*. The men nurse Calandrino back to health; their fee, once again, is three brace of capons.

The last and longest of the Calandrino narratives (IX, 5) is framed in the time it takes to fresco a house: all four of the painters of IX, 5 are summoned to work on a mansion at Camerata, a hill just outside Florence. Such paralleling of the art of painting and the art of deception was foreshadowed in VIII, 9, where Bruno paints the battle between the cats and the mice in the physician's house even as he is duping the physician: 'Shed a little more light up here, Master, and just be patient till I've finished putting the tails on these mice' (52; p. 657). In IX, 5 the painters are joined by another professional illusionist, the prostitute Niccolosa. Calandrino, of course, cannot read her at all (he thinks her 'lovelier than a nymph') but Niccolosa recognizes him instantly as a 'nuovo uomo' (10). 'Uomo' means man; 'nuovo' means new, but also strange, different, unfamiliar (such is Dante's new life in the *Vita nuova*). When Niccolosa rolls her eyes Calandrino falls immediately in love and initiates a courtship that is full of 'nuovi atti' (29; p. 704), strange acts that render the lexicon of courtly love suddenly bizarre. His oaths and vaunts mix the court with the barnyard: 'tell her', he instructs Bruno, 'that I wish her a thousand bushels of the sort of love that fattens a girl' (p. 704; the key verb is *impregnare*, 27). His vision of the end of love sees a mixture of the animal and familial that is almost surreal: 'once I lay my paws on her [le pongo la branca adosso] . . . she'll cling to me like a mother besotted with her son' (36; p. 705).

It is only fitting, then, that Bruno should choose to stage the trysting of the lovers in a hay-barn. As soon as they are alone Niccolosa pushes Calandrino to the ground, gets astride him and acclaims him with a stream of popular love epithets:

'O Calandrin mio dolce, cuor del corpo mio, anima mia, ben mio, riposo mio . . .' (58; p. 708). The barn door bursts open and Monna Tessa (brought from Florence by Nello) sees Niccolosa usurping her accustomed place. She flies at her husband with her nails and tears him to shreds: the animal and the familial come together, but not quite as Calandrino had planned. He returns to Florence and resigns himself 'to the torrent of strictures and abuse to which he was subjected day and night by Monna Tessa' (67; p. 709).

This final image of Calandrino identifies him as the medieval *charivari*'s favourite object of mockery: a husband beaten and dominated by his wife. But no one image can summarize or explain the perennial, mysterious fascination of Calandrino. There is something rustic and archaic in his outlook that begs for policing and so confirms the street-wise modernity of Florentine tricksters and their audience. But he is always more than just a victim of other people's designs: the pleasure in tricking Calandrino lies not in making him follow a preconceived plan, but rather in giving him an unlikely premise and seeing where his own fantastic imagination will take us. Calandrino is himself, we should recall, a painter; his inner landscapes are more fantastic than anything essayed by Maso del Saggio or Frate Cipolla.

Tenth day: magnificence and myths of power

At the beginning of the tenth day Boccaccio's storytellers are already looking to life after and beyond the *brigata* (3; p. 733). But, suitably refreshed by the individualistic, pleasure-seeking format of the ninth day, they soon set their minds to one last effort of collective, thematically unified storytelling. Discussion turns upon those 'who have performed liberal or munificent deeds' ('chi liberalmente o vero magnificamente alcuna cosa operasse'). Before beginning the first *novella*, Neifile likens the key concept here, *magnificenzia*, to the sun shining in the heavens: it is 'the light and splendour of every other virtue' (2; p. 734). Magnificence has a subtle and complex history in the medieval and Renaissance centuries. In Dante's *Convivio* (IV,

xvii) it appears as a virtue defined by Aristotelian ethics as the liberal and reasoned use of great riches. In later centuries the suggestion was made that certain rulers, such as the Medici's Lorenzo il Magnifico and England's Henry VIII (the model for the title role of John Skelton's play *Magnificence*) are walking embodiments of this virtue. Magnificence becomes ever more theatrical; its public staging proves to be an essential instrument of political governance for rulers enjoying absolute power.

Boccaccio's tenth day narratives show a sophisticated understanding of the political dimensions and limits of magnificence. Few men can practise this virtue; impeccable manners and good intentions are not enough. Federigo degli Alberighi, who spends everything he has in wooing Monna Giovanna (V, 9), is not magnificent but foolhardy; he reduces himself to poverty and so removes himself from political life. True magnificence never diminishes the wealth and power of *il magnifico*, but strengthens both (this sometimes requires adroit stage management). Women cannot exercise this virtue since they lack the requisite wealth and power and are too mean-spirited by nature to share what they have: 'you must bear in mind that a woman's heart is not as big as a man's', one woman remarks (9, 30; p. 799); they are almost as tight-fisted as the clergy (2, 4; p. 737). Women play an important part in the theatre of magnificence as symbolic objects transferred between men, although the erotics of *magnificenzia* are exclusively masculine.

Perhaps the purest embodiment of magnificence in the tenth day is Nathan, a fabulously wealthy man from Cathay (northern China) who is evidently modelled on Marco Polo's descriptions of Kublai Khan. Nathan lives in a huge palace by a road that all who pass from east to west, or west to east, must travel; he grows old without ever wearying of dispensing largesse. This excites the envy of a young rival, Mithridanes, who comes to hate Nathan and resolves to surpass him in magnificence. In the course of their struggle Nathan comes to offer Mithridanes his own blood and even his own position in the world. Mithridanes must refuse him since, by the logic of magnificence, he who accepts such gifts recognizes his own subordination. Nathan's only boast is that 'I have never served another living soul', his proof being that 'I have never before taken anything from anyone' (3, 40; p. 748).

When Mithridanes comes to recognize Nathan's greater magnificence, he throws himself at his feet and acknowledges him as 'carissimo padre' (28; 'dearest father', p. 746). No women appear in this third *novella* to complicate its masculine erotics: but even when men begin by seeking a woman's love, they end by recognizing a higher love for their fellow men. In the fifth *novella* (an analogue of Chaucer's *Franklin's Tale*), Messer Ansaldo employs a magician to fulfil the seemingly impossible conditions Dianora sets him as the price of her love (she demands a May-time garden in January). But on realizing that Dianora's husband is willing to let her honour the agreement and sleep with him, Ansaldo finds that 'his heart is purged of the lustful passion' (25; p. 761). His gaze switches to Gilberto, the husband; from that day forth the two men are joined together ('congiunse', 23) in the closest and most loyal friendship.

In discussing this *novella*, the ladies of Boccaccio's *brigata* debate whether Ansaldo, Gilberto or the magician showed the greatest 'liberalità' in 'the affair of Madonna Dianora' (6, 2; p. 762); Dianora herself (who was impeccably loyal to all parties) is not a candidate for honours. A similar pattern is evident in the fourth story, in which Messer Gentile falls passionately in love with Madonna Catalina, wife of Niccoluccio Caccianimico. When the lady dies during pregnancy and is laid in the tomb, Gentile decides to break into the church and steal a kiss from her. But on discovering that the lady is still alive he takes her home and gets his mother to nurse her back to health and then to deliver her of a handsome baby boy. Gentile now conceives of a plan to dramatize his own magnificence by making a gift of mother and baby to Niccoluccio at a public banquet. This requires him to argue (by analogy) that mother and child are his own legal chattels and that he is free to dispose of them as he sees fit: he is not restoring them to the husband (*rendere*), but giving them away (*donare*: 42; p. 755).

Niccoluccio accepts his argument, the drama of magnificence is completed and the two men become life-long friends.

Lauretta concludes this fourth *novella* by commending the restraint with which Gentile controls his fiery passion for the lady ('temperò il suo fuoco', 48). The conquest of individual appetite for a greater social good, an exercise that sees ethics carried over into politics, is exemplified by a number of *novelle* in this final day. The most curious of them is the second, which begins with the Abbot of Cluny ruining his stomach during a spell of easy living with the Pope in Rome. Having set out for the baths at Siena in search of a cure, the Abbot is captured by Ghino di Tacco, a Sienese political exile turned brigand. The Abbot is outraged at being imprisoned by Ghino, but he fails to appreciate that he has come to a place where papal power means nothing, 'and where excommunications and interdicts are entirely ineffectual' (9; p. 738). Ghino, who has some medical knowledge, cures the Abbot's stomach complaint by the simple expedient of putting him on a diet; he then lets him proceed on his way. The Pope, being much amused to hear of all this, makes Ghino a Knight of the Order of Hospitallers and puts him in charge of a large priory. The outlaw and excommunicate Ghino di Tacco (who led a rebellion against the papacy at Radicofani in 1295) is thereby rehabilitated as one who can cure the diseased body of the Church hierarchy.

If this *novella* is read as a political allegory it proves curiously prophetic. In 1375, after a century of loyalty to the Holy See, Florence went to war with the Pope and between 1376 and 1378 defied a papal interdict, thereby becoming a place where (to repeat Ghino's words, translated above) 'le scomunicazioni e gl'interdetti sono scomunicati tutti' (9; p. 738). In fighting this and other wars, the papacy became increasingly dependent on mercenary captains and part-time brigands. In 1377 Cardinal Legate Robert of Geneva persuaded the people of Cesena, who had resisted the looting of his Breton mercenaries, to hand in their weapons. He then sent the English mercenary captain Sir John Hawkwood to join his Bretons in the wholesale massacre of the city: 5,000 men, women, and children were killed in three days. The ease with which the rebel and brigand Ghino di Tacco

is incorporated into the papal power structure in *Decameron*
X, 2 is more disturbing, then, than it first appears: especially
when the *novella* is read in conjunction with *Purgatorio* VI,
13–14, where Dante remembers Ghino for a particularly
savage murder.

Boccaccio's interest in political allegory and myth-making
is most fully developed in the last five narratives of the tenth
day. As his frame of reference gradually expands to accom-
modate the myths of power that structure European and
world politics, the active role accorded to women gradually
diminishes (a fate shared by women today in most grand
theories of political change). The sixth and seventh *novelle*
consider the appropriate attitudes for conquerors to adopt
towards the conquered. In X, 6 a Guelf conqueror, Charles
d'Anjou, falls in love with a daughter of a conquered
Ghibelline and makes plans to abduct her. He is dissuaded
from this by Count Guy de Montfort, one of his closest
companions, who urges him to remember his political responsibilities: 'you are still on a warlike footing in a kingdom
newly acquired, among an alien people, full of deceits and
treachery'; he must not replicate the behaviour of Manfred,
the man he has conquered, since 'it was Manfred's abuse of
his subject's womenfolk that opened the gates of this
kingdom to you'; and he must not plead politics to justify
personal desires by saying 'I did it because he is a Ghibelline'
(28–31; pp. 766–7). Charles accepts Count Guy's advice, provides the girl and her sister with dowries and husbands and,
through prolonged and painful effort, conquers his own
desires: his magnificence is achieved both by what he gives
and by what he gives up.

Medieval political thought defined a tyrant as a ruler who
acts on his own desires rather than seeking the common good,
the *bonum commune*. In 1342, Villani tells us, Walter of
Brienne soon revealed his tyrannical character to the citizens
of Florence by doing obscene things to their wives and
daughters (IV, 17). But love that is controlled through the
decorums of courtly service and kept constantly in the public
domain may actually help a new ruler win over a newly

conquered people. This possibility is brilliantly exemplified by X, 7, in which Lisa, an apothecary's daughter, falls in love with King Peter of Aragon on the very day that he is confirming his conquest of Sicily by acceding to the throne. Fate, the girl insists, decreed that she should fall in love with the king at that very moment (13; p. 770). The king takes the girl's devotion perfectly seriously (without taking sexual advantage of her) and so cures the girl of *amor hereos*, the love sickness that has nearly killed her. At a public ceremony in the apothecary's garden Peter provides Lisa with a husband and a rich dowry and promises to continue as her loyal knight. Lisa, for her part, declares that she 'was always prepared, from the moment I fell in love with you, to make my wishes accord with your own'; she would 'walk through fire' if he commanded her to (42; p. 774). Lisa's timely devotion, in short, proves to be the perfect legitimation for the new ruler. Peter's politics, of conquering hearts by love, are acclaimed by the *brigata*'s ladies as a tactic little employed by 'the rulers of today' (49; p. 775). Peter is a Ghibelline; the ladies are doubtless thinking of the Ghibelline lords of Lombardy who threatened Florence from the north.

The next two *novelle* expand the political framework still further and so reach universal dimensions. X, 8 considers how *translatio studii* accompanies *translatio imperii*, that is, how wisdom and knowledge shift with the epochal transfer of political and military hegemony. The shift observed here is that between ancient Greece and ancient Rome, personified by the Greek youth Gisippus and the Roman Titus: the wisdom that passes between them (the verb is *transmutare*, 38; p. 782) is symbolized in name and in person by Sophronia, a young Athenian girl who thinks she is espoused to Gisippus but (since the Roman loves her more) has actually been married to Titus. Sophronia does not speak once throughout this *novella*, which is moved forward by the mutual love of the Greek and Roman youths and by the death of their fathers. Its centerpiece is the long speech by Titus to the citizens of Athens in which, modulating his philosophy with rhetorical patternings and bare-faced threats, he justifies the transfer of Sophronia from Greece to Rome:

It is true that he [Gisippus] is an Athenian, and I am a Roman. But should there be any dispute between the rival merits of our cities, I would remind you that my own city is free, whilst his pays tribute; I would remind you that my city rules the entire world, whilst his is one of her vassals; and I would remind you that whereas my city is renowned for her soldiers, her statesman, and her men of letters, it is only for the last of these that Gisippus can boast of his.

(67; p. 786)

The ninth *novella* takes on the most fundamental and enduring rivalry of the Middle Ages: the conflict between the faithful and the infidel, Christendom and Islam. Its setting is the Third Crusade (1189–92), a miserable affair which saw the Holy Roman Emperor Frederick Barbarossa drown in his armour and the leadership of Christendom subsequently split between the kings of England and France. The Crusaders' chief objective, the recapture of Jerusalem, was thwarted by Saladin, Sultan of Egypt and Syria, a deeply religious Muslim leader who was much admired in medieval Europe: Dante puts him among the virtuous pagans in *Inferno* IV, 129. Boccaccio's *novella* records acts of kindness exchanged between Saladin and Messer Torello, a nobleman of Pavia who joins the Crusade. Saladin meets Torello as he is travelling through Europe, disguised as a merchant, to assess the Christian state of readiness for the coming conflict. He is so impressed by Torello's magnificent hospitality that he doubts whether Islam can prevail against such men: 'if the kings of Christendom are such excellent princes as this man is a knight, the Sultan of Babylon will be powerless to resist a single one of them, let alone all those we have seen preparing to march against him' (35; p. 800). When the crusading Christians eventually fall into Muslim hands Saladin has the opportunity to match Torello's kindness: he actually envisions the two of them 'ruling as equals over the kingdom I now govern' (73; p. 806). But Torello is obliged to return home because his wife is about to marry another man. Through the magic of Saladin, Torello, dressed as an Arab, touches down in a flying bed at Pavia on the very day of the wedding. The rest of the *novella* sees Torello putting his wife's fidelity to the test; happily enough, she passes with flying colours.

The thought remains, though, that if a Crusader did not have to run home to his wife, the love of two men might have transcended the enduring Christian–Islamic divide.

This ninth *novella* sees a story of magnificence and a myth of power moving in the direction of political fantasy and cosmic fairy-tale. The tenth day's tenth story, being narrated by Dioneo, is typically perverse and deflating: it tells of Walter, a Lombard despot whose behaviour exemplifies not magnificence but senseless brutality ('non cosa magnifica ma una matta bestialità', 3; p. 813). Many readers have been induced to ignore Dioneo's assessment because Petrarch's famous rewriting of Boccaccio's tale as *Seniles* XVII, 3 establishes Walter as a mysterious, God-like figure. But Petrarch, we should recall, spent many years of his mature political life in the service of the Visconti, Lombard despots who (in art, architecture, and their own proclamations) deliberately sought to merge the image of the earthly lord with the Lord above, the *signore* with the *Signore*. Boccaccio, on the other hand, refused all invitations to move to Lombardy and dedicated his political energies to the Florentine Republic. This Republican regime, which was increasingly threatened by Lombard despotism, had established itself just five years before the plague by expelling a tyrant called Walter (Gualtieri), Duke of Athens. It is best to believe Dioneo, then, when he concludes his story by observing that men like Walter are better suited to ruling pigs than human beings ('più degni di guardar porci che d'avere sopra uomini signoria', 68; p. 824). Walter becomes a tyrant (by the logic of medieval political theory) the minute he acts on, rather than fights against, his desire to torture Griselde. His final, theatrical act of public reconciliation, in which he reunites Griselde with the children he has himself stolen from her, is to be seen not as *magnificenzia* but as an obscene parody of it. Such is the fate of the whole lexicon of political virtues when practised under despotism.

The return to Florence and the author's conclusion

At the end of the tenth day King Panfilo commends his subjects for maintaining standards of emotional self-discipline
that Marquis Walter entirely abandoned: rather than yielding
to 'concupiscenzia', they have practised 'continua onestà,
continua concordia, continua fraternal dimestichezza' (4; p.
825). These virtues (decency, concord, brotherly amity) are
essential for the healthy conduct of political life. This does
not imply that the *brigata* has evolved into an ideal political
community or that its individual members have been collec-
tively transformed by the ten-day programme of storytelling.
There are as many signs of faction and division during the
tenth day as there are in the first: one of the female *brigata*
members reveals herself to be a Ghibelline (she cheers for
Peter of Aragon but not for Charles of Anjou) and the tenth
and last *canzone*, sung by Fiammetta, ends in jealousy and
paranoia. And little more is said or done beyond this point:
the storytellers simply retire for the night, get up at dawn and
return to their place of origin, namely the church of Santa
Maria Novella in Florence. The three young men go off 'in
search of other diversions' (16; p. 827); the women return to
their houses.

The tenth day narratives have, of course, prepared us for this
return to the complexities of the political macrocosm. And it is
significant that we have moved from the extraordinary female
leadership of Pampinea in the first day to the routine masculine
leadership of Panfilo in the last. But it is not evident that the
brigata is bringing back anything more or less than what it left
with. The ten Florentines did not leave Florence to seek enlighten-
ment in the countryside: this is a medieval text, not a Romantic
one. What they practise in the countryside is what they bring with
them: an essentially urban capacity for self-regulation exercised
through the sophisticated use of language. When the ten days of
storytelling are over they simply decide to return to the city, their
natural habitat. There is nothing in the text to suggest that the
completion of the storytelling schema signals or coincides with
the end of the plague.

The 'Conclusione dell'autore' which completes Boccaccio's opus offers no clinching moralizations by way of closure but simply brings words to an end: 'tempo è da por fine alle parole' (29; p. 833). In fact, rather than moving us forward, this conclusion brings us full circle: for as the women of the *brigata* return to their houses, they merge with Boccaccio's primary audience of house-bound women. In addressing this short discussion of the merits and defects of his finished work to these women, Boccaccio develops an egregiously complex persona: he is by turns author, literary theorist, seducer, and midnight rambler. He offers sound advice on who ought to read his work, how it should be read and in what circumstances. He also considers his own relationship to the finished work, adopting and then slipping away from the four principal identities a medieval writer could assume (scribe, compiler, expositor, author). But although he is happy to borrow such terms from Scriptural exegesis he ends by insisting that he is writing a vernacular text, not a Latin treatise. The vernacular is the language of experience in the world; the world is never stable but is constantly changing and moving ('sempre . . . in mutamento') and so too is his tongue ('lingua', 27; p. 833). When we first come upon this term 'tongue' ('lingua') we assume it means (stands in for) 'language'. But as we read on in this paragraph we find Boccaccio's 'tonguing' applied to the seduction of a house-bound woman, 'a neighbour of mine', who told him 'that I had the finest and sweetest tongue in the world'. And this links up with his assurance, made a few paragraphs earlier, that although many women have felt his weight (gloss: during sexual intercourse) he is not a man of great gravity: 'I float on the surface of water' (23; p. 832).

Given this extraordinary mixture of bookishness and sexual innuendo, it is not surprising that the work should conclude by repeating the ambiguous, two-pronged rubric it began with: 'Here ends [here begins] . . . the book called *Decameron*, otherwise known as *Prince Galahalt*'. The two-faced text imagines itself, finally, as a surrogate for its masculine author, slipping his way into the houses of Florence and exercising his tongue for the pleasure and solace of women who cannot cross their own doorways and so take part in the greater political world.

Chapter 3

After the *Decameron*

In the last twenty years of his life Boccaccio expressed his increasing dedication to Petrarch and the emergent humanist movement by turning from vernacular composition to Latin encyclopaedism. He wrote just one more text of Italian fiction, the *Corbaccio* ('Evil Crow'), and this may itself be considered as a kind of dramatized anti-feminist encyclopaedia: every misogynistic line on women from antiquity and the Church Fathers to the present finds a place in it. This strange dream narrative, in which an anonymous male narrator learns the terrible truth about women from a ghost, the husband of the widow he is currently infatuated with, may be read as a continuation or revamping of *Decameron* VIII, 7. Boccaccio evidently remained caught between his aspiration for clerical-humanist celibacy and solitariness and his need for female company. He had himself legitimized by papal dispensation in 1360, took minor clerical orders and probably ended his life as a priest. And yet in his Latin vision poem *Olympia*, a remarkably joyful and optimistic work that bears comparison with the Middle English *Pearl*, he meets with five (at least five) of his own illegitimate children who have died in infancy. He was seriously unnerved in 1362 by a message from a Carthusian monk, Pietro Petroni, telling him that he would be damned for eternity if he did not renounce his literary work. And yet in 1370 he set about revising his *Decameron*, producing the autograph manuscript that survives as MS Hamilton 90 in the Berlin Staatsbibliothek.

In 1373, just two years before his death, Boccaccio wrote in humorous vein to his friend Mainardo Cavalcanti, advising him to keep the *Decameron* away from the female members of his household. It is clear that by this time the *Decameron* already enjoyed immense popularity and was moving around the European trade routes with the merchant classes who figure so prominently in its pages. And from this point on the history of the *Decameron*'s European reception becomes a task too vast and complex to even summarize adequately, much less write. Entire monographs have been dedicated to the fortunes of single *novelle*. H. G. Wright set out to write the history of the *Decameron* in England in two years and finished the job in twenty-five: his monumental work has become an inexhaustible well (or bottomless pit) for doctoral dissertations. The Griselde story (X, 10), which has inspired several bad operas and a good one by Massenet, now has an on-going European research seminar dedicated to tracing its labyrinthine diffusion through national cultures. Artists as diverse as Botticelli, Chagall, and Salvador Dali have been moved or commissioned to illustrate scenes from the *Decameron*.

The fortunes of the *Decameron* form part not only of a nation's literary development but also of its economic, social, even religious history. In Italy the first generations of humanists were more willing to praise Boccaccio's Latin encyclopaedism than to admit that they read his Italian prose. By the early sixteenth century, however, humanists and poets were being assured (most famously by Pietro Bembo) that the mission of restoring Latin writing to its former splendour was now far advanced and that the vernacular had been unduly neglected: writers should now emulate the style of Petrarch and Boccaccio, the acknowledged masters of verse and prose. As the humanists turned their attention to Boccaccio, a succession of printed editions transformed the *Decameron* from an alleged entertainment for ladies to a classic text, equipped with the scholarly apparatus of glossaries, grammatical commentary, and historical annotations. In 1557, however, the work was condemned by the Church and placed on its Index. But the anti-clerical qualities that unnerved the Counter-Reformation papacy delighted many readers in emergent Protestant cultures. And as the rest of Europe caught up with the precocious merchant-capitalist energies of mid-Trecento Florence, the imaginative energies of Boccaccio's text seemed to retain the power and relevance of a contemporary text.

The *Decameron* was first translated into French in 1414 by a Frenchman who did not know Italian: Laurent de Premierfait worked from the text of the friar Antonio d'Arezzo, who had translated Boccaccio's work from Italian into Latin. Premierfait's *Décaméron* was commissioned by Jean, duc de Berry; a number of manuscripts from this period contain some exquisite miniatures illustrating scenes from various *novelle*. A new translation, by Antoine de Maçon, was commissioned by Queen Marguerite de Navarre and published in 1545. This new, racy and accurate *Décaméron* provided the immediate inspiration for the *Heptaméron*, a framed collection of tales attributed to Marguerite de Navarre. The condemnation of the *Decameron* by the Council of Trent in 1563 did little to diminish the popularity of Boccaccio's work in France. La Fontaine's first *Contes* were inspired by Boccaccio. Their success emboldened him to write *Nouveaux contes*, in which he tackles some of the *Decameron*'s spicier narratives; these were promptly seized by the police in 1675. William Painter, in his two-volume *Palace of Pleasure* (1566, 1567), was similarly outraged by certain Boccaccian *novelle*: 'there be some . . . that be worthy to be condempned to perpetual prison', he observes (I, 5, 11); sixteen of them are 'redeemed' by his judicious translation and edifying moralizations. Painter worked from the Maçon translation; Shakespeare fashioned *All's Well That Ends Well* from Painter's version of III, 9, probably abetted by one of the eighteen sixteenth-century editions of Maçon and possibly by an Italian edition.

The English *Decameron* arrived somewhat belatedly. The entire work was translated into Catalan in 1429 and fifty *novelle* in Castilian appeared some twenty years later. A German translation was printed in 1473; half the *novelle* were translated into Dutch by the prominent humanist Dirck Cornhert in 1564; the remainder were published in 1605. The first English translation, made by combining a Maçon edition with an expurgated Italian text, did not appear until 1620. Of course, texts and stories from the *Decameron* circulated much earlier than this: Humphrey, Duke of Gloucester, possessed a copy of the Premierfait translation, and the Royal Library of Scotland lists a *Decameron* in 1578. But the most significant witness to the *Decameron*'s influence in England is Chaucer's *Canterbury Tales*. Six of Chaucer's two dozen stories find parallels in the *Decameron*; Boccaccio's influence may be observed both in the general logistics of holding a self-governing group together through storytelling and in innumerable details of narrative technique. Chaucer, whose knowledge of Italian was extraordinarily good, owes more to Boccaccio than to any other writer in any language. He does, however, differentiate himself from Boccaccio by employing a variety of narratives genres where the *Decameron* employs a single, homogenized form: the *novella*. By the sixteenth century, writers in England, finding the variety of juxtaposed Chaucerian forms indecorous and archaic, were more inclined to follow the Boccaccian example; Boccaccio is discovered as a key exemplar for English writing for the second time. The importance of Boccaccio as a source for English writing is recognized by John Dryden in his *Fables Ancient and Modern* (1700), which offers verse translations from a lineage of authors that runs from Homer and Ovid to Boccaccio and Chaucer. Dryden (here and elsewhere) deliberately emphasizes Chaucer's close associations with Boccaccio; the two poets stand very close together in his imagining of the beginnings of the English literary tradition.

The *Decameron* has been most frequently employed by English writers not as a text for translation or emulation but as an inexhaustible fund of stories and narrative devices. In reading a play such as *Cupids Whirligig* (1607), in which Lady Troublesome follows Madonna Isabella's stratagem for explaining away two suitors from her bedroom (VII, 6), it seems impossible to trace the lines of transmission that bring us from Trecento Florence to Jacobean London. But the widespread use of such motifs and devices from the *Decameron* shows that English playwrights of this period were quick to appreciate the latent drama of Boccaccian *novelle*. (Much of this drama is associated with Boccaccio's precocious use of urban and indoor settings.) Nineteenth-century writers tended to favour the more romantic and pathetic tales. Keats, for example, chose to rewrite IV, 5 as *Isabella*, a stanzaic narrative that exploits the gothic dimensions of Boccaccio's original and yet retains a keen appreciation of the hard-edged commercial world that precipitates the tragedy of Lisabetta, Lorenzo's severed head and the pot of basil. George Eliot was attracted by both the romance and the political drama of X, 7: it is evident that she did a lot of homework on the history of King Peter of Aragon. The love-affair between the Victorian English and all things Italian produced much that is forgettable, memorably bad or eccentric. In *Stories from Boccaccio and Other Poems* (1852), James Payn seems determined to turn Boccaccio back into Chaucer: he offers us poetic versions of six *novelle* in a curious variety of metres. The first couplet of the first poem (upbraiding Love for visiting Simona, the humble − but not orphaned − artisan of IV, 7) sets the tone and quality of rhyming: 'How wilful of thee thus to enter in her / Who was but a poor orphan cotton spinner!'

This impulse to rewrite the *Decameron* in a contemporary idiom continues into our own century and has produced two remarkable works in recent years. Pasolini's film *Decameron* (1971) forms the first part of his 'Trilogy of Life', a sequence completed by his *Canterbury Tales* (1972) and *Arabian Nights* (1974). Much of this film's humour is achieved through an egregious splitting of religious and bodily impulses: religion aspires to impossibly elevated and unworldly forms and the body drags us down in pursuit of immediate sensual gratification. In most frames of the film we are either looking up or looking down: up to the convent above the sea, the merchant houses high above the street and to Giotto's idealized representation of the world; down to Andreuccio in the sewer or the well-endowed Masetto sleeping among the vines in the convent garden. Negotiation between these two realms is full of treachery and deception: the many open mouths in the film seem to fill with rotten teeth and bad dental work as the narrative runs forward. The work is framed by the guiding spirit of two characters, Ciappelletto in the first half and Giotto (played by Pasolini himself) in the second. Part One runs as follows: Ciappelletto; Andreuccio in Naples (II, 5); Ciappelletto (and Boccaccio reading IX, 2 in the street); Masetto and the nuns (III, 1); Peronella and the tub (VII, 2); Ciappelletto (a collage of images from Brueghel to signify the journey north, followed by I, 1). Part Two: Giotto (VI, 5); Caterina and the nightingale (V, 4); Giotto painting and eating; Lisabetta and the pot of basil (IV, 5); Neighbour Pietro and the mare's tail (IX, 10); Tingoccio (VII, 10); Giotto contemplating his finished handiwork.

In 1985 Julia Voznesenskaya published *Damskiĭ Dekameron*, a collection of one hundred tales told by ten women quarantined in a Leningrad maternity ward after giving birth and contracting a skin disease. These women come from all walks of life (from shipyard worker and airhostess to dissident and party functionary) and tell stories that range through first love, alcoholism, the threat of rape, Soviet bureaucracy, housing shortages, workers' camps, sex in absurd situations, and the KGB. The ninth day is dedicated to noble deeds and the last to happiness.

Guide to further reading

References to the *Decameron* in this study follow the text in *Tutte le opere di Giovanni Boccaccio*, ed. Vittore Branca, 12 vols., incomplete (Milan, 1964–), vol. IV; this contains good notes in Italian. For the autograph manuscript Hamilton 90, see Giovanni Boccaccio, *Decameron*, ed. Charles S. Singleton (Baltimore, 1974); this includes a facsimile of the coloured sketches with which Boccaccio depicts various characters from his *novelle*. Quotations in English follow the Penguin translation of G. H. McWilliam (Harmondsworth, 1972); McWilliam offers an entertaining account of the follies and evasions of earlier English translators. Charles S. Singleton has updated the John Payne translation of 1886 in Giovanni Boccaccio, *Decameron*, 3 vols. (Berkeley, 1982); volume 3 reproduces the facsimile of Boccaccio's sketches and contains some useful notes by Singleton and his graduate assistants. The translation by Peter Bondanella and Mark Musa (New York, 1982) enjoys a loyal following in the USA.

For a detailed guide to writings on and by Boccaccio in all languages, see Enzo Esposito, *Boccacciana. Bibliografia delle edizioni e degli scritti critici (1939–1974)* (Ravenna, 1976). The periodical *Italian Studies* offers a yearly review of new writings on Boccaccio, and *Studi sul Boccaccio* is the most important forum for new research. For a succinct account of Boccaccio's life and writings, see Anthony K. Cassell, 'Boccaccio', in *Dictionary of the Middle Ages*, ed. J. R. Strayer, 12 vols. (New York, 1982–9), II, 277–90. For a longer account, see Judith P. Serafini-Sauli, *Giovanni Boccaccio* (Boston, 1982); and Thomas G. Bergin, *Boccaccio* (New York, 1981), which offers detailed plot-summaries of Boccaccio's Italian and Latin works. The fullest biographical study is Vittore Branca's *Giovanni Boccaccio. Profilo biografico*; this forms the first part of *Tutte le opere*, vol. 1. The most influential single work of criticism is Branca's *Boccaccio medievale*, 5th edition (Florence, 1981). See also Vittore Branca, *Boccaccio: The Man and his Works*, tr. Richard Monges (New York, 1976) which contains Branca's *Profilo* and some of his most important critical articles.

Other translations, editions and studies of Boccaccio include:

Boccaccio, Giovanni, *The Corbaccio*, tr. Anthony K. Cassell (Urbana, 1975).

Boccaccio, Giovanni, *Eclogues*, tr. Janet L. Smarr (New York, 1987); contains text and translation of *Olympia*.

Almansi, Guido, *The Writer as Liar: Narrative Technique in the 'Decameron'* (London, 1975); a spirited analysis inspired by French structuralism.

Dombrowski, Robert S., ed., *Critical Perspectives on the 'Decameron'* (London, 1976).

Marcus, Millicent Joy, *An Allegory of Form: Literary Self-Consciousness in the 'Decameron'* (Saratoga, 1979).

Mazzotta, Giuseppe, *The World at Play in Boccaccio's 'Decameron'* (Princeton, 1986).

Minnis, A. J. and A. B. Scott, eds., *Medieval Literary Theory and Criticism c. 1100–1375. The Commentary Tradition* (Oxford, 1988); translates from and comments on Boccaccio's contributions to literary theory.

Neuschäfer, Hans Jorg, *Boccaccio und der Beginn der Novelle* (Munich, 1969); compares Boccaccian *novelle* with other medieval narrative genres.

Ó Cuilleanáin, Cormac, *Religion and the Clergy in Boccaccio's 'Decameron'* (Rome, 1984).

Olson, Glending, *Literature as Recreation in the Later Middle Ages* (Ithaca, 1982).

Padoan, Giorgio, *Il Boccaccio, le muse, il Parnaso e l'Arno* (Florence, 1978); includes a number of important pieces, including his seminal 'Mondo aristocratico e mondo comunale nell'ideologia e nell'arte di Giovanni Boccaccio', first printed in *Studi sul Boccaccio*, 2 (1964), 81–216.

Potter, Joy Hambuechen, *Five Frames for the 'Decameron': Communication and Social Systems in the 'Cornice'* (Princeton, 1982).

Scaglione, Aldo, *Nature and Love in the Middle Ages. An Essay on the Cultural Context of the 'Decameron'* (Berkeley, 1963).

Todorov, Tsvetan, *Grammaire du Décaméron* (The Hague, 1969).

For the larger historical and cultural context of the *Decameron*, see:

Alighieri, Dante, *The Divine Comedy*, tr. C. S. Singleton, 6 vols. (Princeton, 1970–5).

Aristotle, *The Politics*, ed. Stephen Everson (Cambridge, 1988).

Becker, Marvin, *Medieval Italy. Constraints and Creativity* (Bloomington, 1981).

Brucker, Gene A., *Florentine Politics and Society 1343–1378* (Princeton, 1962).

Burns, J. H., ed., *The Cambridge History of Medieval Political Thought, c. 350–c. 1450* (Cambridge, 1988).

Capellanus, Andreas, *The Art of Courtly Love*, tr. J. J. Parry (New York, 1941).

Gottfried, Robert S., *The Black Death* (London, 1983).

Larner, John, *Italy in the Age of Dante and Petrarch 1216–1380* (London, 1980).

Meiss, Millard, *Painting in Florence and Siena after the Black Death* (Princeton, 1951; New York, 1964).

Skinner, Quentin, *The Foundations of Modern Political Thought.* Volume One: *The Renaissance* (Cambridge, 1978).

'Ambrogio Lorenzetti: The Artist as Political Philosopher', *Proceedings of the British Academy*, 72 (1986), 1–56.

Smart, Alastair, *The Dawn of Italian Painting 1250–1400* (Oxford, 1978).

Trexler, Richard C., *Public Life in Renaissance Florence* (New York, 1980).

Ullman, Walter, *Law and Politics in the Middle Ages* (Ithaca, 1975).

Villani, Giovanni, *Cronica*, ed. F. G. Dragomanni, 4 vols. (Florence, 1844–5).

Ziegler, Philip, *The Black Death* (London, 1969).

Works which reflect or reflect upon the influence of the *Decameron* include:

Auerbach, Erich, *Mimesis*, tr. W. Trask (Princeton, 1953).

Benson, Larry D., ed., *The Riverside Chaucer*, third edition (Boston, 1987).

Bibliothèque Nationale, *Boccace en France. De l'humanisme à l'érotisme* (Paris, 1975).

Cole, Howard C., *The 'All's Well' Story from Boccaccio to Shakespeare* (Urbana, 1981).

Dryden, John, *The Poems of John Dryden*, ed. James Kinsley, 4 vols. (Oxford, 1958).

Hainsworth, Peter et al., *The Languages of Literature in Renaissance Italy* (Oxford, 1988).

Marguerite de Navarre, *The Heptameron*, tr. P. A. Chilton (Harmondsworth, 1984).

Monostory, Denes, *Der 'Decamerone' und die Deutsche Prosa des XVI. Jahrhunderts* (The Hague, 1971).

Payn, James, *Stories from Boccaccio and Other Poems* (London, 1852).

Pasolini, Pier Paolo, *Decameron* (1971; 111 minutes). Available for rental in 16mm and video forms. Dialects of Italian original are marvellous if difficult to follow; dubbing on English version is dreadful.

Reverand, Cedric D., *Dryden's Final Poetic Mode. The 'Fables'*
    (Philadelphia, 1988).

Sacchetti, Franco, *Il Trecentonovelle*, ed. Antonio Lanza (Florence,
    1984).

Sharpham, Edward, *Cupids Whirligig*, ed. Allardyce Nicoll
    (Waltham Saint Lawrence, 1926).

Snyder, Stephen, *Pier Paolo Pasolini* (Boston, 1980); concentrates
    on his films.

Sorieri, Louis, *Boccaccio's Story of 'Tito e Gisippo' in European
    Literature* (New York, 1937).

Thompson, David and A. F. Nagel, *The Three Crowns of Florence.
    Humanist Assessments of Dante, Petrarca and Boccaccio*
    (New York, 1972).

Tournoy, Gilbert, ed., *Boccaccio in Europe* (Leuven, 1977).

Voznesenskaya, Julia, *The Women's Decameron* (New York,
    1986).

Wright, Herbert G., *Boccaccio in England from Chaucer to Tenny-
    son* (London, 1957).

LaVergne, TN USA
05 February 2011
215353LV00001B/9/A

9 780521 388511